Stefan Abrutat

Wanderer. Warrior.

Chronicler. Twit.

A historical and philosophical
travelogue through the north of
England and Scotland

First published 2016 by Efficacy Publishing

ISBN 978-1533362995

Edited by Shawn Rutledge.

With thanks to Shawn Rutledge, Kristin Marceau, James Heighway, and
Mark 'Corporal Nobby' Baines.

It's about what's over the hill

We're born to move.

Nomads by nature, evolution programmed us to wander, which probably explains why we travel for recreation. What we usually refer to as travelling, however, isn't really. If you think about it, how much of a culture do we *really* experience rushing around in planes, trains and automobiles and staying in resorts and hotels?

Of course, it would be a little naïve of me to think roaming the world on a bicycle could possibly replicate the stresses and strains, or lack thereof, of our nomadic ancestors, but the daily quests into the unknown for food, water and a place to sleep are certainly a lot more in tune with our primary genetic motivators than commuting to cubicles to electronically shuffle virtual paper. The recreation of novelty is built in, so I don't have to tack on artificial pastimes, like skydiving or bungee-jumping, to relieve the stress such sedation accumulates.

And what do we travel *for?* Surely the personal growth that comes from broadening one's perspective? Experiencing other cultures through the window of a hurtling vehicle or cocooned in a lavish resort is never going to reveal the heart of a place, and therefore never really provides that accompanying personal improvement for which we're striving. I strongly suspect those who travel so softly don't do it to intellectually and emotionally experience diversity, they do it for pleasant surroundings, a change of scenery, and a chance to swagger in front of their friends when they get back home. Enlightenment comes more readily, I'm sure, with empathy, understanding and appreciation than a bowl of pot pourri and a pillow mint. We're faking the path to a broader perspective. Building a straw house on a swamp, if you will.

Now this may be a conceit of my own, too. A reverse snobbery of which I've been guilty in the past. In friendly banter, it's relatively easy to verbally and logically destroy an office stiff when one works with one's hands, as I have for 25 years. After all, they're immediately at a disadvantage because their skills are ultimately trivial. They don't physically make anything, so it's a simple transition to suggest they *can't*. In the broader perspective, they're what people who *can* describe as 'useless cunts'. Parasites who piggyback the working man. And the first ones we'll eat when all this comes crashing down.

See what I mean? I look forward to your emails.

I first realized a lot of people view cycle tourists as a little odd when a small town Scottish librarian, while describing the location of a book to a small child, inadvertently whispered just a little too loudly, 'It's on the shelf next to the strange gentleman.'

I suppose I did cut an unusual figure, wearing beige combat shorts over black winter cycling tights, grubby hiking boots, and a startling affront to the cycling jersey industry. A month's growth of beard added an element of destitution, and an unwashed fug established my own political exclusion zone, diplomatically sweetened by deodorant and talcum powder.

This contrasted strongly to a Glaswegian librarian several weeks later, after a tactical shave and wearing more conservative clothing, whom I overheard discussing me with his workmate in conspiratorial tones: 'Oh, he's a writer, you know. Travelling the country on that bike outside after spending twenty years in America!' which made me feel far more professional than I looked, felt, and indeed, smelled.

Bicycle touring is like being cast happily adrift. One ebbs and flows with the day, defined by the bookends of camp and the stricture of sunlight, and the routines of procuring food and water rather than digitally indulging corporate rhetoric. In this sense, I became a nomad, shedding stress and desk pounds as I went. These chores of survival became familiar and comforting rituals. Organization is important, but adaptability is essential, and awkward decisions become less so. Planning is short term at best, and can change on a dime.

It was almost 20 years ago when the idea hit me. Stumbling drunkenly through New York City's Central Park on a Christmas break from university, attired in the student uniform of open fly, coat at half mast and left trouser knee skidded with dogshit, I squinted up at the towering border of office skyscrapers and, surprisingly lucidly given my pronounced irrigation, surmised they would stand empty once this new-fangled internet thing took hold. Virtual offices would come into vogue, and people would work from home. The very idea of commuting, unless one's job had a physical component, would be ludicrous. Office workers would migrate from the towns and cities to live in more amiable village surroundings, with neighbours they could talk to, streets they could walk down and an altogether more pleasing living arrangement. Those remaining urban would re-realize the benefits of neighbourhoods, which would return to mirroring a village's autonomy. Locally owned artisanal outlets and services would re-emerge and flourish, buttressing the sense of community. The importance of friends and family would inch from industrial hibernation.

I proposed, stifling a belch and tripping over a trash can, that we secretly longed for the village: smaller, more cohesive communities typifying our nomadic and early agrarian ancestry. We've spent hundreds of thousands of years in these small groups, and only the last ten thousand or so shifting towards conurbations. So it was obvious to my sottish state, and accurate, later sobriety agreed, that this is where our more evolutionarily entrenched needs and wants could be more comprehensively fulfilled.

However, I recently read 'The Cook's Tale' by Nancy Jackman and Tom Quinn, the latest confirmation of something I'd long witnessed: small, close communities, even artificial ones such as sports teams and social groups, are often plagued by intense personal rivalries and infighting (despite a population of ordinarily calm, educated, intelligent people). Show me any social club and I'll show you a Shakespearian intrigue of imagined insults and simmering mistrust. I think this has to do with perspective: when we can't see the forest for the trees, as it were, it's a lot harder to navigate.

The advantage we would have now is our almost tectonic change in attitude: pervasive access to information has made us much more global-minded and philosophical. Maybe this technology is precisely the evolution we required to separate ourselves from the destructive myopia, or even amblyopia, of extended family communities? Maybe we needed this expansion in awareness to facilitate greater cohesion? Village life with a worldwide perspective. It just might work.

Yeah, so I was wrong about the timeline. Who knew the baby boomer business generation would be so suspicious of change? To this day many refuse to relax their grip on slave galley-like supervision, lording over rows of cubicles like a Roman whipmaster barking orders to the fat drum gimp. And the flood to the village is but a trickle. Sure, maybe the tech isn't quite there yet—we've yet to invent a satisfactory virtual alternative to a face-to-face business meeting, for example—but surely Skype suffices for most interactions?

I decided to go and have a look. I'd visit hundreds upon hundreds of villages and see for myself how the populations were changing. I'd talk to the residents and attempt to gauge whether my hypothesis had merit. It was hardly a scientific study, I hasten to add. Far from it, much more of a good nose around.

This wasn't the sole purpose of the UK leg of my journey. I'd been away from the old country for a long time, and wanted to refamiliarize myself with the land I really didn't know before I left. Plus I needed some exercise: I'd become a full time writer four years ago after a lifetime in construction, so my body, accustomed to burning 5,000+ calories a day, naturally started to thicken around the middle. Vanity has never been enough of a reason for me to work out, hence I brilliantly conceived of this riding and writing project. The promise of a distant castle, or cathedral, or liquid six pack holds me in far greater thrall.

Cycling every day is a joyful exercise, far superior to walking and driving in every way. And I'm not circuitously commuting: every day is a novel journey, where I can stop and write when whimsy strikes, and every night I fall asleep to a different, often spectacular view with a belly bubbling happily over a choice local morsel. Technology allows me to stay off the grid for up to a week, with long-life battery packs to replenish my smartphone, tablet and laptop.

Before I left, and on the early part of the tour, I trilled adamantly to anyone who'd listen that I'm no cyclist and this wasn't about the bike. I fought the pigeonholing like some exotic deviancy, but slowly relented over time as I grew to long for the daily ride. Not because it quelled some carnal urge, you understand, but because I became addicted to moving. I *became* a cyclist, despite my protestations. I still refused to fastidiously record mileages and equipment lists because these were the preserves of the blogging cycle tourist, not the professional writer roaming the landscape searching for meaning. I was being arrogant, essentially.

Anyway, I'll leave you with the words of noted cycle tourist and writer, John Stuart Clark, who puts things so much better than I:

> In shedding the shackles, we are released to be who we are. For some, that can be frightening. The deeper you ride into the back of beyond, the deeper you travel into yourself, gradually experiencing the change of consciousness that ultimately reveals things spiritual. Why else did prophets, hermits and the leaders of the world's great religions enter the wilderness? Ironically, in modern times we enter to escape the inescapableourselves. Yep, it's a zen trip.

In more ways than one, it's about what's over the hill.

Cycling clothes make you look like a pillock

I'm no lover of lycra, you understand, the sheer, air-slick fabric that distinguishes the purist from the part-timer: I viewed the bike merely as convenient transport to wherever took my fancy, rather than an opportunity to dress like a distress beacon. Lumping myself in with the luminous dildo helmet crew would've been woefully longsighted, because they seemed to actually know what they're doing.

I chose to bike because it forced me to exercise, a consideration born of a wish to live longer in order to fit more beer in rather than stave off any chronic infirmity. The more I exercised the more I could eat and drink the delicious things the wearisome said were bad for me; a stubborn commitment to the fleeting spasms of pleasure that make life shiny. I firmly maintained looking slim and fit isn't enough reason to break a sweat, y'see, but if burning a ridiculous amount of calories got me to someplace interesting or something tasty? Hell, let's roll.

I could've backpacked, I suppose, but a dicky hip from years of roofing ensured any loaded hike longer than a few miles reduced me to a lurch straight out of a Romero movie. Factor in a similarly abused lower back and dodgy Texas rugby knees, and cycling suddenly leaped to the fore in ways to carve up a country. I could've driven, but driving separates us from the world. I prefer to be involved, and though cycling is fast enough to get to places, it's slow enough to soak them in.

I wanted to battle the hills and earn the valleys, curse the rain, welcome the sun and exalt the tailwinds. Life, after all, is about experiencing shit, and you don't experience shit motoring along in the air-conditioning. I wanted to nod at rural passersby as if we shared some secret. I wanted to be free. Not American lip-service free or the illusory British version; really, literally, honest-to-goodness, properly free.

I was sure, as I travelled, the inevitable breakdowns and deficiencies would compel me to learn the mechanical minutiae of the bicycle. And I was fairly confident the more I discovered, the more I'd bow to the sage wisdom of the Lycra Dildos, who tended to regard me with either bemusement or loathing. However, this tour was about visiting poignant places and meeting people, not discussing gear ratios, pannier setups, or the best brand of skin tight shorts to aesthetically present one's genitals. More specifically, it was about testing equipment in preparation for the much longer tour to come. Now, maybe I'd fall in love with cycling as I went, but right then I was simply being pragmatic.

I did browse the internet forums while deciding what equipment to buy, but as is usual for these things, the most expensive gear was heralded as the best, especially by people with lots of money. As this was a project I was funding myself, and fully expected to be away from home for many years, I silently dismissed the experts and bought what *I* thought would work, like a truly cheap bastard. Thus I opted for a hardtail mountain bike and single wheel trailer, so single tracks wouldn't prove an obstacle and I could carry more weight. The trailer could be quickly unhitched at a campsite while I rode into town for supplies or if any juicy looking mountain biking opportunities happened along. I added hybrid puncture proof tyres to guard against pointy incursions, toe clips (the old-fashioned kind so I could wear hiking boots, I've never used the cleated type), and bar ends to prevent arm and hand cramps.

Clothing was an awkward choice, because the range of temperatures I'd experience would be extreme, from sweltering to freezing. I went with wicking fabrics because quick drying is important, with fleeces and a tent heater of my own devising to keep me warm. Yes, a *tent*. Some cycle tourists swear by bivvying, opting for the lightweight options to increase their daily mileage. I wasn't particularly worried about covering distance quickly. Plus, if I got caught in days of rain, with a tent I could just plonk myself down somewhere agreeable and work away on my laptop. With the carefully selected electronics I carried, I could last almost a week away from a power socket.

My brother David was kind enough to send me some of his old cycling clobber, citing the lucid notion that the best gear for cycling is, funnily enough, cycling gear. Thus I discovered my objections were actually indirectly aimed at the price tag, rather than looking like a gaudily-garbed ponce. Fascinating.

I had been toying with the idea of a long tour for a couple of years, initially intending to circumnavigate the Mediterranean, but the Arab Spring uprisings put paid to that. Travelling through countries refusing to issue visas was an unattractive prospect, and pretty much all the North African countries were up in arms. It was probably still doable, but the faff wouldn't be worth it. I decided to return to a prior idea, and explore the route of the First Crusade from Clermont in France to Jerusalem, and thence on to wherever: the 'Stans. India. Himalayas. China. The mystery and romance of the Silk Road. (Of course, the First Crusade didn't march from Clermont, but that's where Pope Urban II gave his famous speech, so it made as good a starting point as any.)

I didn't have a specific route in mind, preferring instead to plan only a few days ahead, navigating largely by the availability of resupply and recharging facilities.

My departure was delayed a few times by frustrating logistical and work problems. I ordered a handlebar bag for a second time after it took several weeks to determine the first one wasn't coming, then the second didn't show either. I subsequently found my credit card is limited, for some reason, to nine transactions a day, and both these purchases had been made in the twilight zone beyond.

So I set off on the test tour without one, at the same time hoping a finished ghostwriting project wouldn't require formatting, so I could leave my large laptop at home and just take my netbook to work on. Alas, I had to return ten days later for precisely this reason, and then wait to get paid, which took a month longer than it should've, but provided the opportunity to replace gear that had proved inadequate and buy stuff I hadn't thought of.

I jumped on an amazing deal for a third handlebar bag only to find out too late it shipped from Hong Kong, surface mail. I could have bought another one from a store, I suppose, but I flatly refused to spend the kind of money that would feed me for a month to double up an item I already owned, albeit remotely while it slowly meandered across Eurasia. So that's where I sat for several weeks in near suicidal limbo. Fucking handlebar bags, man. (Yeah yeah yeah, I know, I'm bitching about preparing for a more or less permanent vacation. I'll shut up.)

If the whole notion of travel is to broaden the mind, experience other cultures and foster perspective, we need to see, smell and feel the undesirable expanses between destinations. More importantly, we need to interact with the people who live there. We don't develop much perspective admiring the hotel fountain from a barstool. Well, maybe we do, but that's one I refined years ago. It was time for something new.

It began, as these things so often do, with significant cardiovascular distress.

If mulishness is anything to go by, my trailer, hitherto proving to be a perfectly amenable companion on level ground, objected really quite strongly to being Abrahamically dragged up an incline. The views from the top of the first major character tester, however, made the screaming thighs, gushing sweat and ruptured lungs seem almost worthwhile. This could indicate my character is somehow lacking, I suppose, but I reckon it's not my character that needs work, it's my conviction.

The Vale of Pickering spread inland like a giant picnic blanket, lining the westward valley between the North York Moors and Wolds with a fetchingly florid patchwork of colourful fields, sharply defined by dry stone walls, teeming hedgerows, murmuring becks and ancient copses of twisted trees. It promised the kind of Constablesque cycling landscape I was rapidly beginning to cherish: flat. While my disgruntled muscles made the move from indignant mob to militant trade union, I paused to take it all in. It was a perfect day, the early afternoon sun teasing shadows from the scenery and fomenting a distant haze, framing a view to make the soul take wing.

Too often Brits dismiss the abject beauty on their doorstep for foreign shores, as if they're somehow more tempting, but introduce a visitor from those lands to this and they're invariably stunned by such sights. It's not just the pretty, you understand; it's the lived in. Thousands of years of cultivation tamed the wild, then shaped it. Nowhere else in the world can one see such a perfect synergy of dramatic farmland, epic history and high wilderness, sprinkled with chocolate box villages steeped in the islands' chequered past, but still cosy enough to cuddle.

Having recently returned to my home town of Scarborough from a couple of decades abroad, I saw the old place through eyes unworn by chronological familiarity. Things had changed as much as they'd remained the same. The medieval castle still glowered down from the town's towering central promontory, pugnaciously jutting into the North Sea to split the elegant twin bays. However, new roads and junctions conspired to confound me, and American expressions I thought uniquely my domain now littered local speech. People 'partied' now. They went on 'road trips', drank 'shots', and 'kicked ass'. However, before I sank into despair, my novelty usurped, I witnessed Americans using words like 'ginger', to describe redheads, and 'queue', instead of 'line'. I hadn't noticed this before, probably because I wasn't paying attention, but thanks largely, I suspect, to a little fella named Harry Potter. So, at least transatlantic traffic isn't entirely one way.

My Americanized enthusiasm occasionally jarred with the residents, who were content, as so many Brits seem, to wallow in the joy of communal dissatisfaction. Indignance over local issues dominated eavesdropped conversations, while I bathed in the dialects and marvelled at the elegant turns of phrase. My trains of thought, though, being so often engaged by some lofty background muse (such as tactical vagaries in Call of Duty 4, sandwich ingredient combinations, or Salma Hayek's tits), seemed somehow absently detached from their roundabouts of misunderstandings and disagreements. My opinions, perhaps more often offered than asked, lacked the requisite passion and tact, labelling me aloof and arrogant rather than analytically academic. Unsure how to amend this misconception, I didn't bother trying. Of the two pubs I frequented, the New Tavern in Falsgrave and the Leeds Arms in the Old Town, I was surprised to find myself more comfortable among the working class clientele of the former than the educated, more well-heeled patrons of the latter. Which can mean one of two things: either I'm not as smart as I think I am, or the beer is two-thirds the price.

Scarborough is ringed by the modest hills of the moors to the north and west, and the wolds to the south. Modest, that is, until you pedal up one. Still, the hills further afield were only going to get longer and steeper as they morphed into mountains, so I embraced the training they provided. I started out dismounting and pushing the bike up hills as soon as my legs threatened to form a strike committee, never far into the climb, but by the end of this nine day sojourn I was pistoning up slopes like a lycra locomotive. It's amazing the difference in fitness a mere week makes.

As the sun started to set I rode through Malton, a market town known locally as a refuge for the inbred and malformed. Malton's conurbation includes the village of Norton across the narrow river Derwent, which owes its name to *Derventio*, the first century Roman settlement located here. Visible remains attest to a cavalry fort, which likely first established Malton's reputation as a horse-breeding centre.

The north side of the river tends to be more residential than Norton's industrial south bank, confirming archaeological clues that the Romans implemented this very division, which is quite the 'whoa' moment. As interesting as this is, I didn't want to tarry in the town to discover more, because it increased the risk of engaging one of the misshapen natives staggering around in the open. So, off I pedalled up a long and laborious incline to find my first campsite.

I pitched up in a patch of woodland just off the bypass and settled down with a long-deferred read: Paul Theroux's *The Old Patagonian Express*, a chronicle of his train journey from Boston, Massachusetts to the southern tip of the Americas and bombastically heralded as 'One of the most entrancing travel books written in our time' by the reviewer at the *Financial Times*. I snorted through the first few pages, determined to prove the reviewer wrong, but as I plowed onward Theroux grew on me and revealed a gentler, more romantic soul behind the misanthropic bluster. By the time he got to Oklahoma he'd positively fallen into poetry:

> The land was flat and barren; but the traces of snowpelts of it blown into ruts and depressions, like the scattered carcasses of ermine ... At the topmost portion of the sky's dome, the mournful oatmeal dissolved and slipped, leaving a curvature of aquamarine. The sun was a crimson slit, a red squint in the mass of cereal, a horizontal inch steadied above the horizon.

To alleviate the pressure of comparison I vowed to avoid describing sunsets in my own writing and warmed up a tin of Heinz tomato soup to accompany the roast beef sandwiches I'd brought from home. Minutes later, stuffed with goodness and burping gently, I drifted off to fitfully dream that Sauron's One Eye was, in fact, the sky's vagina, and let's not mention the porridge.

Zen and the art of plastic bag defecation

I awoke desperate for a shit.

I considered breaking camp and backtracking into Malton to search for public facilities. However, none were likely to be open at 5am, and there could well be an early gauntlet of incestuous ignorami and their percussive symphony of glottal stops to navigate. Plus the return would necessitate reclimbing the long hill I'd endured the previous evening. Heading onward into the rolling farmland of the Howardian Hills was also unlikely to produce a result, so I decided to have a first go with my experimental toilet instead. This was nothing fancy: merely a biodegradable plastic bag and wet wipes, but start as you mean to go on, as they say. I folded over the lip of the bag to create enough stiffness to stay open (an old builders' trick), removed my pants, planted my feet wide and squatted like a sumo wrestler.

After a comfortably expeditious evacuation and wipe, I wrung the excess air from the bag, tied a knot in the neck, and buried it nearby using my folding trowel. Remarkably, cleanup had taken but two sheets of pre-moistened toilet tissue (actually one; the second was more of a polish), thanks, I'm sure, to the unfettered delivery posture. There's a lot to be said for this practical but ungainly approach, because 'civilized' toilet seats, by comparison, smush buttocks together like uncooked hams in a freezer bag. Mine were beautifully butterflied out of harm's way: the bogroll budget immediately plummeted and bolstered my beer allotment by a happy fraction. I could get used to this.

Over subsequent days I tried out several stance variations, my favourite being similar to *The Sumo* but with one knee inclined. I tentatively nicknamed this inherently more stable approach *The Sniper* due to its increased accuracy and similarity to the shooting position; however, one does not simply plonk down a knee: experience introduced a lunge-like lean to fine tune the bombing run and prevent splashback, splatter, or dribbling, which can make a terrible mess of the groundsheet.

In remote areas one could always shit outside the tent, of course, but Sod's Law dictates once one is fully committed, as it were, the local Women's Institute dutifully ambles past on their annual picnic. Or a sudden gust of wind casts one in an elaborately feculent caper with the dancing commode. Or even both, if one's karma decides to catch up.

There really is something quite freeing about shitting in a bag in a tent. Most people attach the concept of freedom to owning guns, or the right to roam, or the inalienable expression of an opinion. The problem is these people, more often than not, shit in toilets; the shackles of their subjugation persist. We are no longer in thrall to the plow, or the cotton gin, or the manor house; we're chained to a shithole in the floor. That's the reality, no matter how theatrically it's furnished. Remove this umbilical dependence and the world opens up like a bruised stripper's life story on a weekday afternoon.

Getting over the behavioural hurdle of the first dump is the trick. You'll exploit any excuse and, indeed, go miles out of your way to use more Baroque apparatus, but when you finally resolve to shit into a bag it's like being handed the keys to Elysium. The nonsenses of agrarian civilization—property, ownership, acquisition, jealousy—shudder into sharp relief, then recede from your priorities. You become naturally happier. Food tastes better. The sun shines more warmly, the sky seems more blue. Birdsong cascades with fresh whimsy. You start to see the finer qualities in people, a perception apparently long buried by the childhood rituals of potty training. You cognitively shift to a more streamlined state.

This was extremely surprising to me. I never considered such a small change in mundanity would spark a pronounced shift in consciousness. Who would? Severing that reliance on plumbing immediately fractured a host of anxieties. I suppose it's the same reason people drink alcohol or take other such drugs.

Once you're down with bag shitting, you're never so beholden to towns and villages again. Maslow's widely heralded Hierarchy of Needs poignantly excludes the activity from its level descriptors, which, I reckon, serves to show the invasive effectiveness of Big Porcelain's propaganda juggernaut.

Jeremy Clarkson famously referred to caravan camping as shitting in a bucket in a shed, but he's really inventing disparity where there is none. After all, when you step back and examine toilets objectively, even the most ornately filigreed crapper in the grandest palace is nothing more than a flushing shit bucket. Socially we attach stigma to any plumbing more rudimentary than we're used to, apparently for no other reason than to create a simple snobbery. We actually consider ourselves to be of a higher social rank if our shithole has a u-bend. Shouldn't status symbols be a little more dignified? Buy a fucking yacht if you want to impress people. Jesus.

And how is it nobody spreads the word about this most efficient way of shitting? Surely some people know—the military, for example, has extensive experience in crapping in the woods, but they curiously remain quiet about the benefits. Perhaps they maintain secrecy to foster the idea shitting in such a manner is a hardship worthy of ticket discounts and the occasional free pint? Wikileaks, I have your next exposé.

I would say harden the fuck up, shit into a bag, and see for yourself, but shitting in a bag is quite the pleasure; so rather than perpetuate the hardman illusion our camouflaged contingent so carefully maintain, I fully intend to blow the lid off, as it were.

Really quite impressed with my philosophical discovery, I packed up and hit the road. The first gentle hills provided little in the way of physical challenge, but the scenery improved as elevations increased. Several ruined abbeys and priories decorated the route, glorious bastions of endeavour raised to repopulate the region after William the Conqueror's devastating Harrowing of the North decimated it, but the roadside highlight of the day had to be the Turf Maze of Troy.

I'd never even heard of this thing, and would have been unlikely to stop if not for the elaborate furnishings. There was fencing and a seating area around this room-sized circle of churned turf. Large information signs discouraged the notion it was a quaint practical joke. I dismounted and looked at it for a long while, decided it was a genuine thing (which looked topically like a coiled turd), and buggered off.

It turns out these curious turf arrangements are quite rare, and nobody really knows what they're for. This is one of only eight in the country, and of many more across Europe, especially around the Baltic. This particular one is thought to mirror the ancient maze entrance to the city of Troy, though a popular theory is seafarers would use them to trap any evil spirits following them before leaving on a voyage. This maze's twenty-mile distance from the coast rather upends that notion, however. Still, an interesting curiosity nonetheless, and seeing such curios is what this trip is all about.

I was famished by the time I rolled into the Hambleton Inn at the top of Sutton Bank, palpably looking forward to a good feed, as the food here is borderline legendary. Unfortunately, it is closed on Mondays, despite protestations from Google. Strangling several oaths, I wrangled permission from the landlady to pitch my tent, and made do with a sandwich and another bowl of tomato soup. There's nothing quite so disheartening as being denied something you've been looking forward to all day. And I could've murdered a pint on bogroll credit. Oh well.

Death, broken brakes, and blind luck

I am losing precious days. I am degenerating into a machine for making money. I am learning nothing in this trivial world of men. I must break away and get out into the mountains to learn the news. - *John Muir*

Hares the size of spaniels scattered as I sped along with a becalming breeze. I don't recall seeing so much wildlife in these hills as a youngster, especially of such freakish size, but then I'd never cycled them, nor had I ever really paid much attention. Trips here with my parents were made under duress, way before my appreciation for nature turned up. Indeed, being forced along probably delayed its development.

I also didn't expect to ride over such a variety of roadkill. Of course, there were your usual rabbits, pheasants, grouse and squirrels, but I was surprised to see not one but two otters squashed flat, and a live stoat at one point, darting into the hedgerow. As far as I knew, these latter two species were endangered, so I felt lucky to see them. Well, the stoat at least. But this isn't the 'blind luck' of the chapter heading.

Sutton Bank is a scarp slope renowned for its long and perilous gradient, so much so it necessitates an emergency stopping lane at its base. It is a main road, though, so to avoid traffic I traversed north along the high western edge of the North York Moors before turning down a smaller country lane marked as a cycle route. From this elevation the Pennines rose majestically on the horizon, despite their twenty-mile distance.

This quieter option was a narrow twisting descent that ticked all the right boxes for cycling nirvana. I was only a fraction of the way down the sweeping switchbacks, enjoying myself immensely with the splendid views and tremendous lack of pedalling, when my front brake suddenly faded. Not to worry, I thought, still got the back one. Unfortunately my momentum was so great the now beleaguered rear brake, in horrifying solidarity with the front, followed suit.

I'd been meaning to tighten them both up, but neither set were worn enough to be an issue, or so I'd thought. At least, they likely wouldn't have been without a trailer. The added weight was a dynamic I'd dismissed as trivial.

With brake levers furiously clamped to the handles I plummeted down the cliff, too apprehensive to attempt a controlled crash with the unfamiliar variable of the trailer now monumentally apparent. The turns forced me to bank into corners like a European finance minister, poignantly bookending the Clouseau-like limb-flailing on the straight drops. In desperation, I tried braking with my feet, Flintstones-style, seat nose jammed into my coccyx, boot soles protesting, but the velocity was simply too great. At one point I bore down on a panting lycra cyclist climbing the other way, and, at a loss for a suitably succinct explanation for my grim predicament I shrieked 'morning!' as I rocketed past, twin corkscrews of roaring bootsmoke dispersing in my wake.

I could see what was coming on the straights, but anything could be around the next blind bend, from a motor vehicle to an agitated man with no pants on chasing a plastic bag. I was destined to be either sieved into strawberry jam by a truck grille or face-hugged by a flying sack of shit. By some august quirk of fate, however, on every turn the road ran clear, eliciting a grateful sob and a wonder at which previous kindness was so deserving of cosmic restraint.

And here's the thing: I was hard pressed to think of any. Little stuff, sure, but when was the last time I helped a friend out of a significant fix, or said 'yes' to an invitation? Once one says 'no' a couple of times, people stop asking for either. And why, in this moment of peril, was I speculating about such things? I shut the musing down to deal with more immediate matters, but promised myself further review in retrospect, if able.

The last long straight stretch culminated in a sharp right hander, which would've been the end of man and machine if not for the long, level driveway of a country estate carrying straight on, its gates gloriously, beautifully, fuckably unshut.

Quite taken with my good fortune, I shot up the drive and coasted to a stop, orgasming relief. I dismounted with a wobble and walked back to the road, knees shaking as the adrenaline subsided. Resting my charge against a roadside fence I broke out my shiny new toolkit and started fiddling with the calipers.

I'd purposely bought a bike with disc brakes, as I imagined their increased stopping power would better control the weight. Problem is, I had no idea how they work. Well, I did in principle, from working on cars, but bike brakes are a horse of a different colour. I undid a few Allen bolts, looked at them for a minute, then screwed them back in. There was one bit with a cable running through it, so I unscrewed that, gave it a bit of English and a few exploratory pulls on the brake lever. The caliper didn't close but the cable slid through. Aha, thought I, so that's what that does. I fastened it back up and traced the movement to an internal spring contraption, obviously designed to push the piston against the rotor. After several other such leaps of faith and additional investigative bumbling, I figured out the rudimentary operation but simply couldn't get them to work without grinding; the pads were too worn. Not wanting to damage the rotors, which I imagined would be an expensive fix, I loosened the brakes until they barely caught and continued on my way through some of the prettiest countryside I'd seen so far, longing for a bike shop, a valuable lesson sharply learned.

I figured there'd be one in Northallerton, the small administrative capital of North Yorkshire. I'd been here maybe once or twice as a kid, but certainly didn't recognize the place. I wanted to download the latest episode of Game of Thrones, too, so decided to hole up in a pub for a bit and, physically and figuratively, recharge the ol' batteries.

The beer was cold and cheap, the WiFi strength so-so, but there was nowhere to plug in. I questioned the bartender about this. She said the company that owned the pub couldn't afford such freeloading, so didn't install sockets in the bar area. (I won't mention the name of the pub because I don't want to further damage a business so obviously struggling. Such a move would require a herculean lack of class and tact.) Taken aback, I mused out loud how much it might cost to recharge a mobile phone. It had to be fairly negligible. A penny, perhaps? Two? She shrugged. I Googled it.

The notoriously power hungry iPhone 5 costs about 50p to run for a year. Less than a penny a week, assuming one full charge a day. Less than a seventh of a penny per full charge.

'I'll give you 50p,' I generously offered, to abject refusal. 'A pound?'

'No.'

The Durham Ox

157 High Street

Northallerton

North Yorkshire

DL7 8JX

UK

I think this idea that modern electronics cost a fortune to run (indeed, my father only turns his mobile on to make a call or text, citing expense as the mitigating factor) stems from the days when televisions needed bump starting, and once going would fart and jiggle like a steam tractor, rattling local window panes and showering granny with ceiling plaster. But there really is no excuse for such ignorance nowadays. We all carry these marvellous devices that can instantaneously access pretty much the entire aggregate of current human knowledge, so if you don't fucking know something, look it up.

Rather than decamp and search for somewhere else, I got going. It was such a lovely day my annoyance dissipated as soon as I left the bustle of Northallerton, and that's when I remembered my brakes didn't work. But the land was flatter here, and with no breeze progress was swift, untaxing, and quite lovely in this lull between the highlands. I decided to carry on because screw it. I crossed the A1 (major highway, not the steak sauce) at Leeming Services.

I didn't go into the restaurant and shopping area, but stopped at the petrol station for some sweets. My choices came to be my staple daylong fuel selection for all bike tours hence: Rowntree's Fruit Pastilles and Fruit Gums. Some cyclists swear by Jelly Babies, but they don't know what the hell they're talking about. Jelly Babies are my (and probably your) favourite candy, so much so I rip through a bag like an extinction event. Pastilles and Gums, however, are smaller and by their very nature challenge you to resist chewing, so every sucked sweet is a small success, and life is a game of inches.

Take note, Lycra Dildos.

I also bought a packet of chocolate digestives to have with coffee and a loaf of bread as a soup accompaniment since my sandwiches were sadly dwindling.

The overriding benefit of cycle touring is the ability to eat and drink anything you want, whenever you want, and calories can go fuck themselves. Burning up to 6,000 calories a day means you have to remind yourself constantly to eat. There's a reason professional cyclists are whipcord thin.

To break down what 6,000 calories looks like: that's twelve Big Macs. Twelve. Even the most starving gluttonous twat (me) only manages three.

Or one hundred eggs. One hundred. That's Cool Hand Luke times 2.5.

Fifteen bowls of pasta.

Thirty packets of oatmeal.

Twenty-two of those Southwestern Eggrolls from Chili's.

Twelve bags of chips from a proper British fish 'n' chip shop.

Four 3-piece meals from KFC.

Two and a half large Papa John's pizzas.

Or three cakes. Not cupcakes, folks; proper centrepiece cakes you eat slices of with coffee and ice cream. Hell, a half gallon tub of that only contains 2200 calories; I could eat almost three a day. Lawks.

I continued on through Bedale to arrive at the camping spot I'd planned via Google Maps Streetview, and it was shit. The woodland looked pleasant from the pictures, but they didn't tell me about the damp smelly peat or the outrageously vocal grouse, overconfident while out of season, and obviously agitated at a tent in their midst. I was woken too many times to count by feverishly squawking grouse enthusiastically gang raping this giant nylon interloper.

Oh, how I longed for a minigun.

Poo and candle magic

Despite my best attempts at exploring the philosophical ramifications of my reintegration with the land and people of my youth, I seem to have ended up writing about shit a lot. I don't know how this happened.

I'm not obsessed with bottoms, or their produce, despite all this evidence to the contrary. Please bear with me. It'll end at some point, I'm sure, and I can go on to talk about stunning vistas, colourful flowers, fluffy bunny rabbits and such. Which will certainly make my mother a lot happier.

The morning sun woke the boggy smells first to remind me what a bloody awful campsite this was. The light did slant through the trees rather fetchingly, though, as I stretched the tightness from my muscles. However, this glimmer of a good mood faded when I saw my bike. The nocturnal avian orgy had manifested itself in a bike and trailer absolutely buried in birdshit. I'd propped my rig up against the tree they apparently roosted in, or more specifically, shat from, while watching last night's grouse/tent gangbang. Scat fetishist voyeurs, the lot of them. With acute dysentery, by the looks of it.

I had noticed the forest floor around this particular tree was popcorned with poo, but, like an idiot, I didn't twig what might happen. Another wilderness lesson learned.

Shitty little fuckers.

Revolted but intrigued at what a significant part excrement was playing in this tour only half a week in, I deployed bogroll and spent a good half hour wiping everything down, an inch thick in places, stifling the occasional dry heave.

Not happy with managed wildlife, I generously forwent setting fire to the landscape by placating my vengeful wrath with a Fruit Pastille. I packed and ferried my gear through the woods to the road, hitched up and headed west into the prevailing headwind.

The hills beyond the A1 started to grow. The Pennines of the Yorkshire Dales dominated the horizon, beckoning me on. By mid-afternoon I was well into the national park, a gritty, hot, determined ride through tremendous scenery ending at The Bridge Inn at Grinton, just outside Reeth. Several frosty pints of lager accompanied my social media catch up, but as daylight dwindled I realized I'd have to stay there well into the night to fully recharge my batteries. Needing to find a campsite before proper dark, I said my goodbyes and headed uphill, determined to either roll back into Reeth the next day for the bike shop and all-important brake pads, or continue on to the one in Hawes.

By the time I got to the top, there was no way I was heading back down to Reeth. That's one big, steep hill. The word 'mountain' may even warrant a mention.

I pitched in the heather off a public bridleway with an impossible view and cooked up a packet of random rice slurry. These rice/pasta meals seem to come in one of two flavours; tomatoey or mushroomy. The blurb may well be more imaginative, like 'Mediterranean Tomato & Vegetable', or 'Cheese, Leek & Ham', conjured, no doubt, from the depths of a marketing department doobie, but it's pasta or rice in colourful sand. You have to continually stir the pot to suspend the aggregate in the liquid or it forms a sandbank on the bottom that could beach an oil tanker. I didn't have any 'optional' ingredients like milk or butter, both 'advised' by the manufacturers to 'enhance' the 'flavours' but suggested, I suspect, by their legal counsel to introduce at least one edible component.

I resolved to buy some proper ingredients, and keep this dehydrated muck only for emergencies, but realized my cooking facilities were woefully inadequate. I'd need two stoves, or at the very least a food Thermos for simmering. (It is a strange thing that I'll peruse the packaged foods section in the supermarket, genuinely considering the possibility that this next flavour iteration may well be ambrosia in a bag. I'm always disappointed, and swear off them forever, until a month later when I repeat the process. It's like eating at Taco Bell.)

What? You can cook in a Thermos?! Why yes, you can, as long as it's a good one that retains heat well. You prep them by filling with boiling water, meanwhile bringing the stew or curry or what have you to a steady simmer in a pan. Then empty the water out of the Thermos (preferably using it for some other purpose, like coffee or tea), and pour in the stew, seal it up, and it'll be ready in 6-8 hours, or as long as the Thermos is rated to keep things warm (it's almost impossible to overcook stew, especially by this method). I've got my eye on a one-litre food flask rated for 24 hours, but I'll wait until the weather turns cold before I seriously start looking into regularly preparing hot meals.

By the time it got dark, I noticed it was getting really quite chilly, so I set up my Stef™ ceramic candle heater and unpacked my sleeping bag liner and thermals. (Sleeping bag liners, although gossamer thin, add a game-changing few degrees to a sleeping bag's temperature rating.)

The Stef™ candle heater consists of a tealight candle under an empty soup tin with air holes punched in the top and bottom. Then you upend a terracotta plant pot and set it over the tin, of an appropriate size to nestle nicely, so the top of the tin touches the pot around about its middle.

The candle heats the tin, which heats the terracotta, which retains the heat and warms the tent. If your hands get cold while you're outside, you can warm them directly on the pot when you get back in. It's like a hand warmer for a shelter.

A tealight candle costs what, a penny? Four to five hours of warmth for a penny. I like these numbers. And once lit, it was warm enough in the tent to hang out in just a t-shirt, despite dropping below freezing outside. Obviously, you have to make sure your tent is large enough to avoid accidentally knocking it over, and I always put mine in a far corner on my small chopping board so it doesn't bugger up the groundsheet.

I didn't invent the idea, though; I reproduced another model I found online consisting of three pots of diminishing size nested and held together by a thick steel bolt running through the holes in their bases, with a small stack of washers separating each pot. This arrangement needs to sit on some kind of support in order to get a candle under the metal; a couple of bricks set at a right angle, for example. Unfortunately I found it to be incredibly inefficient, despite extensive experimentation with different configurations. Eventually I discovered less metal was better, because it heats up quicker and transfers heat more efficiently from the candle to the pot, which is what you really want, and after much ciphering and head scratching, arrived at the current lighter, simpler, design.

Pleased with my toasty abode, two episodes of HBO's *Kill Generation* failed to close my eyes, so I fired up that trusty Shakespearean standby: *Coriolanus*. I've never made it past the twenty minute mark with this movie before collapsing into a snoring, twitching heap, and tonight it proved its worth once more.

However, I was awoken throughout the night by a perpetual conversation taking place outside the tent between, by all accounts, Chewbacca and the Predator. Throaty mewls and groans danced with percussive trills and roars. Hollywood should seriously look into grouse for alien vocalization recordings; their range is enormous, loud, and quite otherworldly. Just grab one, stick it in a cage and poke it with a stick.

I'll happily volunteer as the stick man.

The excruciating pedantry of officialdom

I rose to frost so thick it looked like snow—no wonder the wildlife was bitching—the water bottle on my bike was frozen solid. Minus 3°C in May? What the hell? I decided this would be a good time to stay in my sleeping bag and have a rest day to let my knackered body recuperate from the ravages of the previous days' cycling. When it got warmer I'd fiddle with my infernal front brake a bit more, so I watched a couple of movies and breakfasted on coffee, chocolate digestives and a vitamin tablet.

I *would've* stayed all day, that is, if two clipboards hadn't turned up on an ATV and declared I wasn't allowed to camp here. Some early morning hikers had dutifully reported seeing a tent. Imagine that, a tent in the middle of nowhere! Fuck me, alert the media.

Two things bother me immensely about this. First, realizing there are people who think someone sleeping in the wilderness warrants intervention from the 'authorities', and second, those 'authorities' enthusiastically agreeing with them.

Aside from the obvious immorality of attempting to curtail such natural freedoms, there's a whole legal grey area here I want to explore. If the right to roam allows us to traverse ancient pathways established over long centuries, indeed millennia in many cases, despite the ever-changing land ownership and political climate, are we not 'allowed' to stop and rest at any point, on a public right of way? If so, for how long are we 'allowed' to rest? Ten minutes? An hour? Is someone going to time us? Will we get arrested for sitting down to eat a sandwich? What about lying down in the heather for an afternoon nap, *Last of the Summer Wine*-style? What about lying down in the evening for a snooze? Why not just stay 'til morning and leave then? Who is it hurting? And who establishes these parameters? And who gives them the right to, ultimately, physically altercate with us to stop us from doing so? I think the answer may well be to tell them to piss off and mind their own fucking business, and if they attempt to physically remove us, defend ourselves. These *individuals* are initiating a personal confrontation, no matter how thick the clipboard paperwork arbitrarily granting them permission to do so. They're human beings sticking their oar in, not arbiters of heavenly justice righting the wrongs of property abuse. It really would be a better idea for everyone involved to just leave everyone else alone.

Of course, the landowners point of view is they don't want their land, crops or livestock damaged. Well, to normal people, that goes without saying. The last thing any reasonable person would do is damage another's livelihood. But what about those who will, you ask? Prosecute *them* for damages, not all of us. Introducing blanket rules to exclude the innocent majority because of a few inconsiderate idiots is the kind of misgoverning that leads to brutal revolution. It's like banning all sitting because someone took a shit.

Yes, it's exactly like that.

I had made a couple of fundamental errors in my 'wild camping' (as 'camping' is now called, I suppose to make it sound more edgy for the kids) by pitching in sight of a trail and not leaving at first light. I resolved to start looking for campsites earlier in the day from now on, so I could more covertly select locations. Do I dislike having to do it this way? Yeah, but it's far less hassle than having to roundly beat officials up every morning, which neatly avoids consequences like grave descriptions on Crimewatch and countrywide manhunts.

I quizzed the clipboards about the legality of their objections. Their primary concern was fires, which is fair enough, I suppose (I didn't have a fire), but when they started on about erosion and environmental damage, I had to interject. I didn't say anything, but I did look meaningfully at my bike, then levelled a stare at the chunky tyres on their four-wheeler. Their arguments trailed off, slightly embarrassed, as well they should be. All I leave behind is flattened grass and the occasional buried biodegradable bag of shit. If anything, I'm actually fertilizing the countryside, causing more good than harm. Now then, what are *you* doing by comparison? Shooting birds?

The grouse population has to be managed or there won't be enough food for them...'

'Because landowners chopped down all the trees and killed all the predators. Tell me more about this environmental conservation.'

'It's not that simple.'

'It's not. Neither is physically trying to impose your will on someone bigger than you for no other reason than attempting to enforce an arbitrary rule some twit made up in London.'

Realizing they were losing this one rapidly, they changed the subject and suggested they were going to involve additional officialdom of a more medieval demeanour armed with truncheons. I generously agreed to leave.

I climbed further onto the tops and saw far more concealed opportunities for camping I could've exploited if I hadn't been so tired yesterday. Oh well. Stopping to rest by a spring, I used my Travel Tap water filter for the first time, essentially a water bottle with a filter in the cap, which purports to eliminate every dangerous pathogen. I filtered enough water to fill up my two litre main bottle and half-litre bike bottle, feeling very Enid Blyton.

It was really starting to warm up into a beautiful day, contrasting starkly to the bleakness of the rolling moorland and early chill. I pedalled across the tops peeling off layers, thoroughly impressed with this entire bike touring malarkey. This is what it was all about: an easy ride through dramatic scenery without a clipboard, stopwatch or nerdy office rubber stamp twat in sight.

When I started to descend into Wensleydale, I realized the folly of not returning to Reeth to get my brakes looked at. With such massive descents spreading over many miles, I was forced to dismount and not push, but pull my rig back from hurtling down the incline as I progressed valley-ward. The bonus was more time enjoying immense views, as a working bike would've meant slamming down this hills at thirty miles per hour for an entirely different jolly.

I turned right on the way down to head to Castle Bolton, because it's a castle and I'm a history whore. As I rode into the village I saw an untended tablet computer on a bench on the green. A Kindle Fire, it looked like. I knocked on a few nearby doors to no avail, until I tried a larger house further afield and bumped into the homeowners sitting outside, enjoying the sun and the view from their position on the side of the dale. I explained what I'd found, and they promised to hand it in to the truncheon men. I declined the offer of a cup of tea, immediately regretting doing so—I've got to stop doing that, my deeply ingrained English wish to avoid being a bother seriously hampers my networking ability—and set off to inspect the castle.

Bolton Castle was built between 1378 and 1399 by Richard le Scrope, a famous knight who fought at the renowned French battle of Crecy under the Black Prince in 1346. His name also sounds a little like 'scrote', which is tremendously funny to my juvenile sense of humour and suggests Richard

(Dick) may have been 'A Boy Named Sue' tough. It also hosted Mary, Queen of Scots for a while.

The castle is currently run by the heir to the 8th Baron of Bolton, a Capt. Hon. Thomas Peter Algar Orde-Powlett MC, recipient of a 2003 Military Cross in Iraq, and now, more than likely, someone who harasses people sleeping in tents. I didn't get to meet him, so I'm probably judging unfairly, but it's a relatively well-preserved castle with some pleasant gardens and a maze, which are to his credit.

With the wind now at my back I hurried on through Wensleydale, passing through the village of Carperby and its Wheatsheaf hotel, where James Herriot himself spent his 1941 honeymoon. I was trucking along so well I declined to stop for a pint, which isn't like me at all.

Wrestling my rig down one particular hill outside Hawes, I came upon a couple of farmers rebuilding a dry stone wall knocked down by a car some weeks previously. I watched them work and chatted with them for a while, fascinated by the skill set; dry stone walling is the one construction trade I've never had the opportunity to learn. They gave me directions to the bike shop in Hawes, which subsequently turned out to have closed down a couple of years ago. I doubt they knew.

I got on Google Maps and found another bike shop at the far end of the village, which dropped me at the Youth Hostel. Weird. I decided to wait the couple of hours for them to open at 5pm, and see if they had any bike parts to sell, perhaps explaining their Google Map reference. They didn't, so it didn't. Fuck.

Okay, do I continue on with no brakes? Bumbling around mountainous country visiting non-existent bike shops (that, I later found, were unlikely to carry the pads I needed anyway) was rapidly wearing thin. I decided to backtrack to Leyburn, the largest nearby town, and see what was available there.

Rocks and plots and sex in the dales

With the day beginning to wane at 5pm, I had no idea where I was going to sleep, having inadvertently neglected to plan beyond Hawes. Invigorated by this unknown, I rolled back into the village centre, bought some vegetable soup and fresh bread from the small supermarket I'd seen, then headed east. With the sun at my back, I cruised down the A684, tracking the river Ure.

I've never liked cycling on major roads since a car hit me from behind about a decade ago in America. My bike went under the car, I went over it. Nothing broken but bike, skin and dignity, yet the next day my body felt like it'd been gleefully dismembered then viciously kicked back together. As my job at the time was very physical, I was off work for over a month. I had to undergo four weeks of physical therapy and two courses of pain meds and muscle relaxers, which was easily the stuporous highlight of the year (which is saying something, because I like to get my stupor on quite regularly). I didn't get much of anything done that month, but by Odin, it was fun not doing it. Since then I've shied away from cycling on busy roads when there's a sidewalk, and fully intend to keep doing so. The law can bugger off.

If I'd thought about it, I'd have headed up to the tops to camp, but thinking is for the unweary. I stubbornly put my head down and grinded out mile after mile looking for somewhere suitably discreet.

I passed a hillock on my left at one point, obviously man-made and ancient, surmounted by an apparently purposeless stone wall. With no mention on the map and no one around to ask, I resolved to enquire about this curiosity in the next village, with the faint hope of obtaining permission to camp there so I could investigate further.

I wobbled up the climb into Aysgarth on dying legs, but was immediately distracted from my quest by the Aysgarth Rock Garden, a ridiculously modest name for such a stunning tumble of boulders. This seemingly haphazard jumble is to regular rock gardens what Bradley Wiggins is to, well, me.

The new owners were just leaving after a maintenance session, but I managed to persuade them to give me a quick tour. What followed was as pleasing a dawdle as one could hope for. Adrian and Rosemary went out of their way to guide me through their rocky warren, explaining the alpine flora they tended and the history of the habitat.

There's something tremendously antediluvian about this manufactured grotto. It tapped into that primitive satisfaction one feels as a child after building a particularly well-concealed den, an emotive reward no doubt evolved to counter predation. Very fetching and cosy, with hidden coves, aesthetic nooks, a spring-fed pond and well-placed benches that must be heaven to exploit on a summer's day with a good book and a frosty beverage.

I must admit, I was a little disappointed to discover it wasn't a natural phenomenon; maybe some freak moraine; where prehistoric priests could've cobbled together romantic yarns about ice giants kicking pebbles into a heap, or a lovers' retreat moulded by the hands of a pervy old Earth Mother.

Ah, the despair of missed bullshitting opportunities.

It is testament to the workmen's skill I didn't immediately twig the telltale signs of artifice, but the first stone lintel over an archway eventually gave it away. The garden was commissioned at the turn of the last century by the eccentric owner of the cottage opposite (now Heather Cottage, a pleasant-looking B&B), one Frank Sayer Graham, and built by a firm from York, sixty miles distant, over a period of eight years. The massive boulders were dug up on the surrounding highland and transported down by horse-drawn cart, a feat I could doubly appreciate with my newfound respect for brakes and steep hills.

Frank had quite the story: his father, Francis Sayer, was a farmer who lived in the same cottage and used the pre-rockery plot as a kitchen garden. In what I'm sure at the time was quite the village curtain twitcher, he impregnated Elizabeth Graham, his housekeeper half his age, and she moved in. They never wed.

Goodness me.

After his death in 1871, she and Frank continued to live here until he married and she moved to another house in the village, only to pass away shortly thereafter.

Frank made his living as a fur trader, cultivating the commercial rabbit population on Ladyhill, just up the dale. The luxuriant silver-grey fur of these rabbits was in such demand for the lining of expensive car coats he made a fortune, enough to afford two live-in servants (here we go again...), and his pet project became the rock garden. But not as a public work, oh no, only for him, his wife and invited guests (incidentally his first wife died when she was 45, so he went on to marry her *sister*. Aysgarth is rapidly starting to resemble an uncensored episode of *Up Pompeii!*).

Local children, especially, were discouraged from exploring the site, which is remarkably selfish, because the childlike mindset is precisely what finds this kind of thing appealing. But then, with this family, I shudder to think what went on within. So maybe the exclusion was a singularly moral move by the dirty old codger?

After *his* death in 1946 it eventually fell into disuse and grew over. Luckily, the owners previous to Adrian and Rosemary spent a few years rescuing it from the ravages of nature and opened it to the public. Quite chuffed with my discovery I said goodbye to my new friends and headed on, the mysterious mound and wall completely forgotten.

It was seriously getting dark before I found the perfect field to camp in: no gate, no farmhouse in sight, no crops, and a stone wall high enough to hide me from the road. I settled down for the night and dreamed of giants.

(Sorry, that's poetic bollocks. I actually dreamed of three uncharacteristically agreeable ex-girlfriends all at the same time. Just as things were starting to get nice and Aysgarthian, a passing truck woke me up. Cursing, I exasperatedly made a quick note to buy some earplugs.)

From top to bottom

Aside from the hopefully paused rather than deleted dream orgy, I had a wonderfully uninterrupted night of sleep. I breakfasted, decamped, and was on the road by 5.30am. Now *that's* how wild camping is supposed to bloody go! I didn't once have to shake the tent to dislodge amorous fowl, or attempt to decipher extra-terrestrial chatter, or threaten a single obstinate clipboard with thinly-veiled violence.

The rising sun came at me sideways on the empty road, diffused by the loitering mist in the lowlands, but bathing the sparsely treed upland slopes in stripes of warmth and colour. Perfection. I enjoyed a couple of quiet hours cycling through scenery that'd cause even the most workshy poet to stop fiddling with himself and scrabble for a thesaurus.

I switched off the audio book to bask in the silence and solitude. With no one else up this early, it was all for me. Right then, I was the only person in the world. Yeah, so I'm an indulgent twat. Like you haven't figured this out yet.

I'd been listening to Dan Carlin's *Hardcore History* podcast as I rode these past few days, and they were a revelation. Each podcast is essentially a short audio book, where Dan makes intelligent historical connections to illustrate the foibles of the human condition. Fascinating conversation fodder. I can't recommend him enough.

On this tour I'd also started listening to David Mitchell's *Cloud Atlas* and had to stop after the first few minutes, because I was struck immediately this was something I needed to read in print. Really good writing has to be read, I think, because print reading is a serial consideration; one gets to pause and ponder at leisure, and review a phrase, sentence, paragraph, or chapter as necessary. Audio books don't allow this luxury quite so easily; they spool inexorably onward, especially when one's pedalling in traffic, rectum bellowing like a Jango Fett seismic charge every time a heavy goods vehicle thunders close. You can't just whip out your phone and press 'pause' on a whim. And even then, I wouldn't want to. I want to see the wordy juxtaposition as it's designed to be seen. Old-fashioned, me.

When traffic finally did show up in the ones and twos common to rural areas, to a car they were Land Rovers or Range Rovers. The difference, my wall-building buddies had informed me, was 'new' farmers versus 'old'. New farmers, apparently driving the Range Rovers, are a gentle, useless lot. Chinless and inbred, they'd spent time at schools 'papa' had to pay for, all the while being roundly buggered by their classmates. They recoil from building dry stone walls, which is why these skills, like so many others, are being lost. They're land managers, not farmers. Land Rovers, on the other hand, are driven by the old school: real men in patched wellies with holes in their jumpers, gaps in their dentistry, and pensive proverbs but a wistful scratch away. These are the only two options, I was reliably informed, and it was obvious to which group this salty brace belonged.

While these sweeping demographics exhibit a certain distain, I couldn't help but ascribe them an element of truth if driving habits are anything to go by. Land Rovers would typically potter along behind me until I could find space to let them pass, when they'd do so with a cheery wave, or even stop for a chat. Range Rovers acted more like minicabs at an airport, with every overtake oozing hostility. Of course, it could just be me underlining my confirmation bias, but it has to be said.

I do enjoy the enmity exhibited towards cyclists by some drivers, because deflating ignorant entitlement is a particularly satisfying pet project of mine, to road space or anything else. I understand some cyclists are becoming increasingly militant about careless driving, as an uncountable number of YouTube videos attest, but I'm of a more aggressive mindset, especially with such a hefty bike lock. Yep, riding a bike allows you to carry an offensive weapon. Mine's about three feet of heavy duty industrial chain in a fabric sheath, held together by a weighty padlock not much smaller than my fist, stored in a frame bag just in front of my saddle. It's one helluva game changer. I haven't had to pull it on anyone yet, but I'm itching for the day just to see how much damage it'll do, I mean, how much of a deterrent it is.

I do understand, of course, that I'm incriminating myself by announcing an intent to use my bike lock as a medieval flail. It's a curious wobble in English law that many objects aren't deemed offensive weapons until one uses them so, or expresses an intent. (Odd lot, English lawmakers. Anyway, pretend I didn't say anything or I'll belt you with it.)

There is, of course, a third group: the Range Rover driver slumming in a Land Rover. These stealth fops are difficult to identify until they start to speak. And it's just then you'll notice their artificial dishevelment: the flat cap is jauntily askew rather than indifferently placed: corduroy trousers held up by a belt instead of rope: the Barbour crumpled because it fell off the hook by the kitchen AGA, not a result of sleeping in a field on the way home from the pub last week.

There are those who say it's only the working farmers and the ridiculously rich who drive the Land Rovers, because they're similar in not giving too much of a fuck. Range Rovers are for people in the middle, who struggle for identity between the two. I have to say my experiences so far support this notion.

Leyburn proved to be a dead end for brake pads, so that was the end of that. I'd have to head home. I did actually have a supplemental motive; I had some formatting work to finish which is far more doable on the large laptop I'd left behind than the little netbook I'd brought with me.

I dismounted and pushed up the hill into Middleham, a hillside town of 850 people, 500 race horses, 4 pubs and a castle. It was mid-morning, so I stopped for a rest on the village square war memorial, fought the urge to move here permanently, and watched a couple of hours go by. The number of horses clopping through the streets to the exercise fields was extraordinary.

I've never seen so many in one place. Skittish lot, too, these thoroughbreds. Village squares don't come much quieter than Middleham, but the horses apparently hadn't been informed.

Their eyes darted about, widening at every novelty. Riders struggled to stop their charges stampeding at the merest wisp of a threat. Have we done this to these animals with our selective breeding? It's difficult to imagine any beast so teetering on the edge of frenzied panic ever surviving long in the wild. I toyed with the notion that if these psychotic clusterfucks were the product of induced inbreeding, it explains a lot of people in government.

I noticed a public lavatory and scoffed at the idea. Amateurs. It was next door to the chip shop, so I waited for them to open for lunch and treated myself to battered sausage and chips before mounting up, no longer considering the word 'thoroughbred' a compliment.

Google told me Ripon had a library, so I set off in that direction for the recharging facilities. About 2 in the afternoon I was getting knackered, so I started looking for a campsite. It was a long look, ending at a small patch of woodland about 4.30pm. It wasn't perfect, being a little too close to the road, so I carried on for another 20 minutes, couldn't find anything better, so gave up and doubled back.

I relaxed in my tent, fired up the latest episode of *Kill Generation*, and set the mosquito coil outside to deflect the emerging hordes of midges, only to watch an actual mosquito fly in and land on the tent wall, looking as surprised as I was. What the fuck? In Britain?! I'd never seen one in the UK before. I looked at it, it looked at me, so I backhanded it like a shortchanged pimp.

What the hell? Since when has the Old Country had mosquitoes? We've always had midges: clouds of invasive little buggers who camp-follow hikers and like nothing better than kamikaze attacks on eyes or mouth, nipping skin like tiny terriers when they miss, but mosquitoes? I guess we really are in Europe now.

I zipped up and spent a pleasant evening with *Kill Generation* until nearby gunfire roused me from a snooze. People were hunting in the woods, but I figured I was close enough to the road to be out of danger.

I bedded in and went to proper sleep. It turned cold again, however, and I woke shivering. Rather than break out the heater, sleeping bag liner, or extra layers, I pulled my fleece in through the sleeping bag breathing hole but couldn't be arsed to put it on, falling back asleep immediately.

Now there's a neat trick I didn't know. When it turns cold during the night, there's no need to open up the warm cocoon of your sleeping bag to augment your layers; simply pull in a sweater. It fills up the empty space and, in this particular instance, kept me warm until morning.

It also began to rain for the first time on this tour. There's nothing more cosy than being in a tent during a rainstorm, yet this is the thing that apparently puts a lot of people off camping. What a strange lot.

Rolling home

Did not want to get out of bed this morning.

After seven days of robust physical activity, especially after months (some would say years) of nothing more strenuous than elbowing pint glasses through a well-groved right angle and the occasional Greco-Roman bout with a stubborn pub door, I was knackered.

I needed a rest day from all this bloody exercise, cumulatively compounded by struggling down every mountain slope as well as pushing up its contrary antecedent. Thanks to irrepairable brakes, my cycling tour had morphed into something usually sponsored for charity.

There are those who say one should train for things like this: build up some core conditioning to prepare for the lung-busters. I'm not one of those people, I get bored too easily (I suspect most people think the same, which is why all this go-for-it motivational behaviour is so prevalent among the 'work out' crowd). For me, doing is the practice, and I'll recover as required. Unfortunately, this 'required' bit couldn't be catered to: successful wild camping necessitates moving on in the morning, as yesterday had proven. I swore down tomorrow I would rest, determined to find somewhere remote I could lounge for a while and work on sweet bugger all. I prepared for another long day in the saddle.

Saddles are important equipment for the touring cyclist, as well they should be—no one cherishes a groin sore. Thus the market is awash with bum support technology, and the cream of the crop are the British Brooks saddles: old-fashioned leather numbers that mould to one's hindquarters over time. No new technology even remotely compares, and global confidence in the brand is literally overwhelming. The plastic gel saddle that came with my bike became painfully debilitating after the first couple of hours into any long ride, so I plonked the sixty-odd quid down for a Brooks, and it blew me away. Even without padded cycling shorts, I never had a problem. Here on tour, the last thing I ever thought about was pressure on the ol' perineum.

I've since discovered a company called Spa Cycles in Harrogate who make identical Brooks copies for half the price; the price Brooks saddles used to cost before they took off in America.

After so many days on my lonesome, punctuated by engaging interactions with country folk, I was shocked by the spralling conurbation of Ripon. Hardly a large town, and often thought of as visually fetching, I disliked every street and indifferent pedestrian. As soon as you enter any conurbation you have to remember to stop acknowledging passersby, but with Ripon, for some reason, I felt the transition even more starkly than usual. It's a curious thing that the more people around, the less we interact. The entire population of 16,000 seemed to be out choking the streets, so much so I had to dismount and navigate the narrow thoroughfares to the library, which, like many libraries, just happens to be right by the bus station.

The first words spoken to me in Ripon were from a startlingly ugly teenage girl in a gaggle of contemporaries 'chillaxing' on one of the bus station benches. I say 'teenage' because that's the age she looked to me, but I'm no zoologist. 'Giz a go on yer bike, mate?' She ooked, eliciting appreciative chatter from her subordinates.

From my egocentric perception, the monkeys were taunting the silverback. To them, I was a target. I don't know if it was her casual disregard for civility that annoyed me, or the realization that I must look like an utter wally in my cycling get up, or that verbally admonishing today's children is a thankless task typically culminating in loud accusations of pedophilia. Best left well alone, I shrewdly thought. But then I suddenly entertained the idea they'd get hanged up the road in Hartlepool (the population of Hartlepool have been locally ridiculed as 'monkey-hangers' since the Napoleonic wars after a dead monkey washed ashore. They hanged it for being a French spy. The fact it was already dead didn't appear relevant), as they bore a remarkable resemblance to, perhaps not dead monkeys, but certainly deserving of at least a *National Geographic* cover. I toyed with the idea of tossing a banana onto the appropriate bus and buying four tickets northeast. Significantly cheered by this notion, I nodded knowingly at the smirking simians as I locked up my rig, and swore to myself if I saw, through the library window I'd strategically parked in front of, any of them knuckle over to the bike racks I'd speed this doomed evolutionary oversight to its inevitable conclusion.

In the library I discovered there was no WiFi. But of course! This is Ripon, after all. Relieved to find a connected electrical socket and even one or two unchewed books, I charged up for a few minutes and spent my time unsuccessfully attempting to tether to my phone's data connection. This being a Saturday the library closed at 2pm, so thereafter I fought through the crowds by the somewhat plain cathedral and headed to the river to fill up on water, discouraged by civilization in general.

The rest of the day was spent on a very pleasant ride east with a helpful tailwind. As dark approached I bought half-a-dozen free range eggs from a farmer's roadside honour stall, and camped down in some remote woods to a dinner of Bachelor's Chicken & Mushroom Pasta, poaching three of the eggs in the sauce as the pasta was almost done. I wolfed it down with six slices of bread. Nothing to shout about, but dining al fresco after a day of hard physical work always tastes better for some reason, and I was looking forward to a day off tomorrow.

'Who gave you permission to camp here?'

'Didn't know I needed any,' I replied evenly, soothing his glare with a grin. The farmer had driven his Land Rover slowly past my tent earlier that afternoon, set back into the sparse pines off a dirt road, and returned with a minder. The newcomer was a big man, but like the smaller farmer, well into his fifties. 'I didn't see any signage or fencing.'

'There doesn't need to be any. You're only allowed to camp on established campgrounds.'

Horseshit. The British people wouldn't allow politicians to strip away their rights to enjoy nature so, would they? Besides, no goddamned way was I sharing a field with the shrieking kids, shitting dogs, obnoxious drunks and suspiciously ungypsy-looking gypsies that typify a commercial site. I made a mental note to Google this new assault on personal freedom the next time I achieved a phone signal. 'Since when?'

'Since the Right to Roam Act. No camping anywhere without permission.'

'Sounds very 1930s Germany. I've been living abroad for the last twenty years, y'see, so I'm a little behind on the more recent rounds of the government's immoral legislative villainy.'

The farmer pursed his lips, apparently warming to this dig at authority. 'How long are you planning on staying?'

'I'll be gone at first light.'

'I don't want to see any fires.'

'I cold camp.' I don't, but I wasn't going to give this miserable twat a reason to make me exert myself in a physical altercation. I'd cycled 40 miles yesterday, fully loaded through hilly, twisting terrain with no brakes, so was in no mood for smacking around old people.

'How do you cook your food?' piped up the minder, suddenly inspired.

'I cold camp.' He quieted, obviously confused by the cunning repetition.

Changing tack, the farmer asked the minder if he was going hunting in these woods tonight: a tediously transparent attempt at shotgun intimidation. Barely stifling his enthusiasm for the opportunity to scare an unarmed 'townie', the minder told me to beware of noises in the night and how I should keep my head down if I knew what was good for me. I chuckled at their thin charade and purposely made no overt move towards my very, very itchy bumpkin-slaying hatchet. Instead, I forced out something congenial and uninflammatory. They went on their way. What a pointless waste of interaction.

I spent the rest of the day watching movies and relaxing in general, finally enjoying some respite from the grind. Take away something as simple as the downhills and cycling becomes exponentially more of a chore.

I was up, packed and gone by 7.30am, dismissing the urge to shallow plant a loosely-tied bag of shit as a booby trap for the farmer's inevitable return. I rode through the Howardian Hills to Malton, on a route I'd never in my life traversed before. The amount of lovely scenery, regal country estates, and jigsaw-worthy villages was truly surprising.

Once through Malton, I hit the A64 cycle path, put my head down and was home by lunchtime.

For a group that's so looked down upon by a significant portion of the motoring population, the cycling community is really quite fractured. I noticed this as I trawled for tips on the touring cyclists' forums. Ordinarily when a group of people is faced with prejudice, they band together in a cohesive solidarity. Not cyclists, though.

I've always associated snobbery (or any other kind of prejudice) with useless people, and the overwhelming majority of the time I've been proven correct. The idea that a motorist is somehow superior to a cyclist, or one type of cycling is more worthwhile than another, is absolutely ludicrous, and the preserve, quite obviously, of the coward. To look down on someone exerting real physical effort to get around in an as environmentally friendly fashion as possible only serves to confirm what an honestly expendable sack of shit is doing the driving.

I did notice a recent trend of cyclists wearing helmet cams to record traffic infractions that put them in danger, then loading their videos to YouTube. Many of these auteurs seemed to actually pursue confrontation rather than politely give way to two tons of vehicle, which tends to be my more discerning modus operandi. I decided against wearing one, as I'd prefer to have as little evidence as possible when forced to drag a raging motorist through his car window for an etiquette refresher.

I must say, though, I didn't experience a single instance of road rage, or even a horn beeped in annoyance. The occasional car did pass too close for comfort, but I credit that to ignorance more than malice.

Yorkshire is big. Far bigger than I credited, and breathtakingly beautiful. I mean, I knew it was going to be fantastic to look at—I grew up here—but memory proved to be a poor reference.

Twenty years of Texas scrubland and desert had ill-prepared me for the uncontrived friendliness of the people (towns discluded), the sheerness of the landscape and, of course, the depth of the colour green.

I also learned what equipment worked, what didn't, and which bits became invaluable. I'd been surprisingly accurate in my pre-tour predictions, so there wasn't much to discard as I prepared for my far longer trip to Scotland a couple of months later.

Pirates, cannon, and barrels of piss

I haven't always had a sweet tooth. I used to be able to go for months without looking at sweets or cookies. I've forgone cake for years at a time. A new girlfriend once expressed concern over an impulse buy of several bumper packs of candy, only to marvel when they sat unopened on the sideboard six months later.

Not now, though. Now I hunt for sugar like a prowling night terror. Cycling did this to me.

In the saddle, one needs a steady supply of energy, and sugar is the most portable delivery system. I'm into the habit of snacking on Rowntree's Fruit Pastilles and Fruit Gums, but I'll occasionally foray into Jelly Babies when I'm feeling particularly pleased with myself, or if I'm flush with cash. This is because I tear through Jelly Babies with the same genocidal zeal seen in comic book villains and the enthusiastically religious. My average m.p.j.b. (miles per jelly baby) currently stands at 'haven't got any back to the bike yet'.

Tactically loaded with rolls of pastilles and gums, I left in the late afternoon so I didn't have far to ride before camping for the night, shrewdly easing myself into the exercise to avoid suffering stiffness the days after. I knew where I was going to pitch my tent: an old alum quarry on the disused Scarborough to Whitby railway track, now a bridleway that could frankly use a little attention from a maintenance crew.

I'd watched a documentary on the quarry the night before, so I was excited to revisit a place I'd known since childhood, but this time armed with a little history to jimmy the imagination. It's about ten miles north of Scarborough, but I'd overestimated my pathetic cardio, arriving well after dark, huffing like a glue sniffer and cursing my inadequate bike lights.

I ignored the 'no overnight camping' signs because I refuse to acknowledge such inarguably immoral rules, quickly set up my tent and settled down to an evening of sandwiches, movies, and satisfaction at finally having set off.

The morning was afire. Beneath my lofty vantage point, the broad sweep of coast from Ravenscar to Robin Hood's Bay silently basked in lazy corals, decadent blues and warmest gold. The world was drunk on summer.

I can quite shamelessly say I've never seen anything so beautiful. It was so ridiculously pretty I actually chuckled. This magnificent sight encouraged me to linger, so like a proper libertine, I did. I waived breaking camp and went for a wander.

The ruins of the eighteenth century alum processing buildings sit a ways down the slope from the despoiled cliff face, where men chemically extracted the alum before packing it by mule and pony down the towering cliffs to the rocky beach. They even carved a harbour from the solid stone shore. The sheer industry in such an endeavour boggles the mind; these men *worked*.

This huge slot berthed Whitby Colliers: the same sturdy flat-bottomed ships used by Captain Cook (who grew up a morning's walk from here) to explore the far sides of the world.

The flat keel meant they could be beached for loading the processed alum, and unloading barrels of piss used in the process from as far afield as London, and coal for the furnaces, and seaweed from the Orkneys: a rich source of potassium.

This unassuming but rugged stretch of coast was largely responsible for the European discovery of Australia, New Zealand, Hawaii, and the North West Passage. The alum was also similarly instrumental in kickstarting the industrial revolution and the hunger for empire... let me explain.

Alum is used as a mordant to 'fix' dye in wool so it doesn't immediately wash out, as well as to soften leather, fireproof cloth, make paper smooth, and stop bleeding. In the late medieval, all of these things were pretty important, as you can well imagine. The all-powerful Vatican of the fifteenth century monopolized alum production throughout Europe, so when Henry VIII told them to bugger off, the British were cut from the supply. This forced their vital textile industry to rely on shipping cloth to Belgium for dyeing, whose alum, it is said, was inferior and expensive. Thus, when huge local sources were discovered in Yorkshire during the early seventeenth century, the entire island mobilized to exploit it. Something so trivial and seemingly innocent, from such an isolated and desolate place, significantly changed the face of the world. Forever. I've always loved peering into bottlenecks, especially historical ones. Not sure why.

The shale quarried from these cliffs is rich in aluminium silicates and iron pyrites (bear with me, folks, this could get fucking boring). Alum was formed from combining the sulphur from the pyrites with the alumina from the silicates. The start of this complicated process (remarkably discovered through trial and error) was to burn the shale over brushwood fires, in great heaps called 'clamps' often approaching a hundred feet high. After a time, the chemical reaction produced enough heat to fuel itself, and these clamps would be allowed to smolder away for up to a year, turning the rock a red colour.

This 'calcined' shale was then soaked in vats of water to create an aluminium sulphate liquor, which was stored for a while in settling tanks before being drained off down long stone channels to the Alum House a few hundred feet below.

The exhausted shale was then unceremoniously dumped in huge mounds near the quarry, now a preferred habitat of hardy gorse bushes.

Once in the Alum House the liquor was boiled and mixed with either potash (from the seaweed) or ammonia (from the piss) to reduce acidity, and allowed to cool. Alum crystals would form, which is what they were after. The liquor could be boiled several times to maximize the yield. At its height, the operation garnered around two tons of alum per day.

So valuable was this stuff there was a real threat of attack by pirates, so the clifftops were armed with cannon.

Pirates, cannon, and barrels of piss. Chemistry just got interesting.

Happy as a squirrel with three nuts I set off for Whitby, enthused by discovery, encouraged by the industry of folks I'd never meet, and thoroughly impressed that my British adventure was set for compelling heights if I'm making such finds a mere hour's ride from home.

On the way, I came across a loose horse on the track. We pretty much surprised each other, and he cantered off away from me. I had to head in the same direction, so I followed him. This little procession lasted for a good ten minutes before he decided he was far enough from home, and tried to figure out how to turn back without getting too close.

I stopped and shimmied over to the side of the track to give him as much room as possible, but he still pushed through the undergrowth on the far side instead. Domesticated horses are pretty fucking stupid.

Turning left at Whitby I headed up the Esk Valley, where the sharp slopes found my legs sorely lacking in steam. I spent an hour pushing up inclines too steep to pedal, most notably the unpaved (and extremely rough) Straight Lane, which used to join the medieval hillside village of Aislaby to its twelfth century riverside mill. The mill was dismantled during the 1800s so I didn't bother searching for it. (Another even older mill is to be found at Ruswarp, where I'd crossed the river a mile or two seaward. I recently discovered it had been owned by my grand uncle-in-law. I'd ridden right past it and didn't even know. Spooky.

Climbing out of the valley onto the moors, I encountered a large group of cyclists on a circuitous day's ride from Pickering. They stopped for a chat and polite marvel at the trailer. One or two of the older men were a little dismissive of my plans, which I took to be envy, and openly criticized my rig, saying panniers were the better way to go. I danced around the conversation, managed to avoid telling them to fuck off, and didn't punch anybody. Positive result all round, I feel.

What is this bitchy infighting thing in cycling? I'm not used to this veiled aggression, I'm used to sharp wit and bloody knuckles. Maybe tight shorts cut off circulation to the balls or something.

I eavesdropped on two old dears in the pub chatting over a photo album: 'She spent four grand on her teeth, y'know. Two month later, she were dead.'

I never mean to snot beer across the bar, because of the mess it makes. Bartenders have a thankless enough job as it is, dealing with the likes of me after a few jars, so to compound their duties with mopping up an overspill is really quite ungrateful. I made my apologies and helped him clean, all the while straining my ears for further gems.

'She's dead. She's dead. He died of cancer. I think he's alive. No, no, let me think. No, he's dead.'

I absolutely lost it with the giggles. These two were perfect Yorkshire caricatures. Scarcely believing my luck, I drunkenly repaired to the campsite and wrote this down, because I knew I would forget the particulars in the morning.

I'd never been to Hinderwell, which sounds weird to say because my Scarborough primary school was similarly named, so I was intrigued as I rolled in. Quite a pretty village with a great artisanal butcher and a lovely campsite called 'Serenity'. Very friendly folks, and I was the only camper there, so I had the entire field to myself. I took the opportunity to reorganize the way I packed my gear, as after camping last night, glaring inconveniences became apparent.

The ducks from their duck pond came calling in the morning, obviously tamed by more charitable campers chucking out breakfast scraps. I love duck, especially with pork stuffing. I decided they'd miss one and issued a reprieve. They probably had names.

I stayed for two days to get some work done and charge up, aided by their comfy 24-hour WiFi cabin. Wise move, because it rained the entire day. I dashed to the chippy that night for sausage and chips, deftly sidestepped some predatory local women looking for a shag, then reconsidered the wisdom of my agility back at the tent. Oh well.

I'm particularly bad at 'seizing the day'. My first instinct is to say 'no'. I've got to learn to say 'yes'. And I'm not just talking about orgies in remote villages named after my primary school, I'm talking about life in general. One should be enthusiastic and encouraging, even when one doesn't feel it, because the recipient certainly does. And the recipient is everything. Unless, of course, one's a selfish cunt.

Pork, packing, and ghosts of the past

I spent the morning reorganizing my packing.

The last couple of days revealed some glaring inefficiencies in my haphazardly-loaded trailer. I needed a systemized hierarchy of likely sequential need and to better utilize the small panniers I'd been reserving for food and cooking equipment. Plus I needed to focus more weight towards the front of the trailer to prevent fishtailing on the downhills. This took an hour or two, then I went shopping for the legend that is: the 500-year-old Cumberland sausage.

Of course, like an utter twat I completely forgot about the artisanal butcher shop down the street, and instead biked a mile or two to the Co-op in the next village over. There the Cumberlands disappointingly came packaged in links instead of the traditional continuous coil. To be expected, I suppose, but far from authentic.

The sausage got its name from the extinct (though recently revived, probably by some worrying genetic legerdemain) Cumberland pig, which Wikipedia describes as having 'an upturned snout and ears that flopped forwards'; certainly sounding like every other pig I'd ever seen. What set Cumberland sausage apart from its contemporaries was apparently the unique flavour profile of the Cumberland pork, which was traditionally roughly chopped rather than minced, and heavily seasoned thanks to the confluence of the spice trade in Whitehaven during the 18th century.

Butchers in Cumbria had been pursuing Protected Geographical Status for a while, which would afford their product the same label exclusivity enjoyed by Champagne and Parma ham (but sadly not Texas chilli).

Protected Geographical Indication (PGI) was eventually granted in 2011 for the name *Traditional Cumberland Sausage*. This applies only to those produced in Cumbria with the appropriate seasoning, unlinked, and made with more than 80% meat.

I stowed the knock-off Cumbies for the next night's dinner so I could take advantage of Hinderwell's chippy, which turned out to be perfectly passable fare alongside a tasty pork pie from the butchers.

I set off the next morning in mist, drizzle and an unseasonably cold September wind. I wrapped up and dug deep to grind over the punishing Upton Hill, then swept into downtrodden Skinningrove, and wished I'd taken another route.

I don't know if you've ever played the creepy video game *Silent Hill*, where the protagonist is trapped in a deserted town shrouded in mist containing strange, lurching creatures, but this was a lot like that. Most of the houses I could see through the gloom were boarded up, derelict since the ironstone mines closed in the seventies, and the cold fist of doubt gripped my rapidly shrinking bollocks.

Silence.

Not a car to be seen. No barking dogs, no singing birds, no people about. It was *The Walking Dead* with a sea fret. Unfortunately, the semi-abandoned village is in a steep coastal river gorge, so the climb up the cliffs opposite was an arduous one; I had to dismount and push. Shady figures occasionally emerged from the ominous brume to watch me struggle past, like zombies staring at food they can't reach. Not a one talked, or even moaned. I put my head down and kept pushing.

Exhausted by my escape but refreshed by the sun peeking through the thinner clifftop mist, I started hunting early for a place to camp, but didn't find anywhere suitable until late afternoon. Tucked away in a forested corner on the outskirts of Saltburn-by-the-Sea, I stumbled upon the ruin of Marske Mill, just off the Cleveland Way. There's been a mill on this site since 1649, and it stayed in use until the 1920s.

Much like the Straight Lane from Aislaby, it's a steep descent while one's wrestling a bike and trailer to save the brake pads. It was too muddy and rocky to ride, which allowed me to appreciate the effort required by folks to get their grain down to the mill before combustion power turned up. A farm apparently occupied the site afterwards, but was demolished in 1971. And now here was I, alone and about to sleep with the ghosts.

At least I would've been alone. While I was settling down to watch the next episode of *Battlestar Galactica*, ruminating on how people from a different star system manage to get their hands on Cuban cigars when they've never been to Earth and don't know where it is, a courting couple turned up and and started quietly arguing. She was obviously breaking up with him, and he was attempting to dissuade her by bringing her to this local beauty spot.

The guy needed to give it up. Once women get to that stage the relationship is already over. Hidden in my tent, which itself was out of sight, I willed him to bail, but he persisted in pursuing previously unplumbed levels of cringing indignity for a couple of more hours.

Meanwhile, back in space, Starbuck accidentally shot Apollo in a bar gunfight. Jesus fuck, is this woman the Rhamnusian nemesis of the Odama family or what? She'd already got the other son killed by neglecting his flight training to play with his Cumberland. I almost called out to the bickering lovers, '*See what happens? Let her go, man! IF YOU LOVE HER,*

YOU'LL LET HER GO! She sounds like a bitch anyway,' but I got distracted by wondering how the main characters all have definitive jobs—pilot, marine, engineer etc, but nevertheless end up doing everything else themselves. The crumbling narrative outside faded into meaningless babble as I realized *Galactica* pilots were leading special forces operations, ground assaults, spy missions, mechanical maintenance, scientific research, search and rescue attempts... is everyone else really so shit at their own jobs they've got to put the generically good-looking people in charge? What message does that send to our butt ugly kids? Oh, that's right, we don't have any.

I made Cumberland sausage sandwiches for dinner (along with one of my personal weaknesses, Heinz cream of tomato soup) and they tasted much the same as any other pork sausage. I decided they were far from the genuine article and resolved to sample from a more reliable source.

I pushed back up the hill at 8am, all my gear still wet from the previous day, but the sun warmed me as I got to the top. Saltburn's quite scenic when you can see it, I mused, as I left through the affluent quarter and headed for Redcar.

I stopped at a petrol station to buy a Coke and a Lion bar, then rode to a high coastal viewpoint to breakfast on them. Two kids cycled up on their BMXs and quizzed me about my rig, and I took not insignificant pleasure in basking in their unfettered admiration.

Afterwards I dropped down the hills to the flat coast road, buffed with sand dunes, and stopped at some public bathrooms to fill up on water and have a nose around an MG car rally in the adjacent car park. I took some pictures, said hello, and buggered off into Redcar.

The last time I'd been to Redcar was on a fondly-remembered minibus trip about 25 years ago to watch The Stray Cats play a reunion concert. It'd been a dump to rival Skinningrove then, but they've prettied up the place in the interim.

I stopped to take some pictures of giant wind generators in the bay, when an old fella with hiking poles and a Texas baseball cap (I lived in Texas for almost 20 years) stopped for a chat. Turns out he had a daughter living in Katy, Texas, which sounds quite cute until you discover it's an area of Houston, the Birmingham of the Gulf Coast.

This old boy walked six miles every day to stay in shape. He was 83. We talked for a good half hour before I managed to tug away, and I can't for the life of me remember what about. I do recall some mention of a son living in the south of France. He recommended I look him up when I go through there. It's highly unlikely I will, but touring, I was beginning to discover, is peppered with such generous offers, transforming one's faith in humanity. The broad strokes of travelling in such a way means you meet more people you aren't circuitously paying to be there (guides, accommodation and transportation staff, service personnel, etc), so there's a less perceived difference in status to spark hostility.

I hit a very new-looking cycleway into Middlesbrough. The city looks like they're trying to keep up with Redcar, but have a ways to go yet. I joined the path west along the Tees, one of northern England's great industrial rivers still echoing with the thunder of empire, now an easy ride through not unpleasant countryside. I was to turn north in Stockton-on-Tees, but had a hard time finding the correct path, and Stockton is not a town to get lost in. I drifted through some veritable war zones where gangs of roaming youths gawked predatorily at me. I mean mugged back, which must've looked ridiculous while dressed like a lemon lollipop wearing a cock helmet. I became hyper aware of the threat, unzipping my frame bag for easier access to my hefty bike lock, and dangling a handful of chain out so it was easier to grab, just in case.

There was no problem at all, of course, and I eventually found the bridleway and set off at a fair clip, hampered, however, by the increasingly common anti-motorbike gates. Not a problem for people on regular bicycles, but the trailer proved a hindrance. I was philosophical at first about unhooking it to get through, each transition taking a couple of minutes (I had to grab one of my telescopic hiking poles, set it to the required length, prop my bike up with it, carefully unhook the trailer, walk the bike through, prop it up again, get the trailer through or over, hook it up again, retract and stow the pole), but after the thirtieth in a day I could've quite happily visited the Cleveland town planning office with a loaded shotgun and a bottle of Drano.

The upside of having to stop so often is you get to meet a lot of bridleway users, most of whom want to chat, particularly other cyclists. I talked with one experienced rider for twenty minutes or so, and he gave me a wealth of advice about where to go in Scotland, the routes to take and things to see. We rode together for a bit and parted ways at a crossroads. About an hour later he caught up with me with an old saddle to replace the one I'd just spent a significant portion of our interaction bitching about. He'd dashed home to fetch it and then must've put in some seriously hard work to catch up, because I wasn't particularly dawdling. What a nice chap and a lovely gesture. Absolutely made my week, that did. I switched saddles immediately and my backside has never been more grateful. That saddle saw me home, where I could order a proper leather touring saddle from Spa Cycles in Harrogate. (Leather saddles are the most popular choice for long-haul tourists, because they mould to one's backside over time, like a pair of shoes to one's feet.)

While this bridleway ran for a good thirty or forty miles to Seaham, I couldn't find a single discrete place suitable for a tent. Finally a cyclist commuting home from work told me of a likely site on the shores of Hurworth Burn Reservoir in County Durham about an hour ahead, which turned out to be a perfect spot, and one I would've likely ridden straight past. I hung all my wet stuff on a gate to dry overnight and lit my candle lantern in the tent to take the edge off the chill.

Poachers, gypsies, and ducky boys

As I was breaking camp a poacher and his dog came up the path. Bloody hell, I thought, a *poacher*? What the Downton Abbey is going on? He must've been out overnight because it was just getting light and he was toting a brace of rabbits. He asked if I had any water, so I gave him my bike bottle and said he could keep it. I needed to buy a bigger one anyway and I didn't particularly want to swap lip muck with this grubby fucker. I only spied a single tooth and it looked to be on the verge itself.

I've nothing against poaching or hunting in general, and don't particularly distinguish between the two. The idea of someone 'owning' wild animals, even managed ones, is biospherically silly, and my years immersed in the lingering frontier mentality of the southwestern USA forever changed my attitude to killing one's own food. I'd now prefer to do it myself for ethical reasons (I look forward to the letter bombs from outraged vegans), and will probably start at some point on this trip, but there was something 'off' about this guy. I've no doubt if he'd happened upon my camp while I was asleep he'd have stolen something. He was probably measuring me up to see if mugging me now was doable, hence the weird vibe, but obviously decided it wasn't.

I've got several friends, mostly vegans, who disavow hunting as if it's the preserve of bloodthirsty nature haters. But the thing is, hunting is what *nature does*. It's as natural as birdsong. Pretending it's somehow cruel is to imply we're above animals, whereas I contend we are not, or at least, not much. Thus theirs is the more arrogant position.

I don't often engage, because it's rarely worth the effort. The vegan establishment necessarily rides roughshod over the science, cherrypicking for their agenda as they go, very much like the fundamentally religious. Even when you categorically prove them wrong, you don't win, because you're tearing down their psychological safe harbour, which never feels good. They imagine a refuge of fluffy bunny rabbits, anthropomorphized dolphins and gaily frolicking lambs, whereas in reality nature has teeth and claws and blood and death alongside the genetic altruism. It looks attractive to us, though, because we're supposed to be in it, so we often forget its rigour. Nothing wild dies of old age; only we do. Nothing is designed to live into infirmity.

Veganism is the weirdest and most fascinating behavioural mutation of modern humanity, and it's occurring right before our eyes. I guess one's opinion of it depends on how far one thinks we've drifted from our hunter-gatherer roots. I suggest, psychologically and physiologically, we haven't moved much at all; we haven't had time. 10,000 years is but a stutter in our storyline. Which is why, I think, we're so miserable in the monogamous agrarian domesticity that breeds the veganism outlier. Stress-related illnesses are the biggest killer we have. For comparison, cross-cultural studies abound with happy and comparatively stress-free immediate-return hunter-gatherer societies.

So why did we choose agriculture if we hate it so much? No doubt because it's easier. Put a dog in a house and he lies by the fire.

Any herbivore versus omnivore debate ultimately arrives at *sentience*. Animals are sentient, is the most frequent claim, and plants are not. This is murky territory and fairly redundant, certainly for the hungry, of any species. Life eats life. Making guesstimations about the level of sentience of a life form is, I feel, cultural navel-gazing. These classifications are derived from our facility with language, not because nature, our *implicit* nature, recognizes such things.

I'm with the vegetarians when it comes to the mistreatment of farmed animals, however. Like most people, I don't want to see anything suffer, plants included. And if this fuels your objection to consuming the derived animal products, well, good for you, and please don't stop on my account.

There are bad days (Skinningrove), good days, and amazing days. Today was the latter. The first part of the day was spent winding through rolling hills. I noticed a lot of single horses tethered seemingly in the middle of nowhere, likely by gypsies. The horse grazed a circle around the anchor, which was then was moved to a different part of the common or field, if the patterns of cropped grass were anything to go by.

There was a village up ahead, so I stopped to ask a middle-aged man cycling on the bike path if there was a village shop where I could stock up on food, water and candy. He said there was, and he'd show me, and warned me the place was a 'bit rough'. So rough, in fact, he refused to enter, and gave me directions from the outskirts. What the hell? It was only 10 o'clock in the morning.

Wingate appeared to be distinctly removed from Ducky Boy territory, but the residents were having none of it. I leaned my bike on a lamppost outside the general store, unlocked but in plain view of the shop window, and went in to grab what I needed. 'I wouldn't leave your bike there,' advised the shop assistant when I got to the counter, 'they'll have it, y'know. Before you even blink.'

A headscarfed old lady in front of me turned in agreement, 'She's right, luv. Buggers, they are.'

There's a few reasons I knew the potential for theft was unlikely. First, I have a length of slip-knotted paracord I use to tie my front brake lever back, as I found the weight of the trailer could easily unbalance while propped up or leaning against something: applying the front brake stopped the wheel from rolling when it turned. The side effect is anyone trying to snatch the rig would have to work this 'parking brake' out and fiddle with it before setting off, by which time I'd be on them with ferocious, violent, bone-snapping prejudice. Second, while it only takes a couple of minutes to get used to the trailer (indeed, once moving it's barely noticeable), the first time, at low speeds, it feels very strange. Third, all my gear is strapped on and everything valuable is in my small backpack. Fourth, any self-respecting career hooligan is still in bed at 10am.

I returned to my never-out-of-sight bike to find it miraculously still there, when a baker in a white apron walked past carrying a huge tray of freshly baked pork pies. What the Dickensian? This *is* Downton bloody Abbey! The smell was heavenly, and before I knew it I was trotting after him like a cartoon dog. He took them up the road to Robinson's Butchers, a bustling craft-oriented local shop with an obviously stellar reputation. I joined the queue inside and acquired one, still hot, to rival the legendary pork pies of Glaves Butchers in Brompton-by-Sawdon.

I sauntered through Seaham and Ryhope enjoying a following wind along County Durham's coastline, which impressively combines the qualities of being both pretty and easy to cycle. I did a little more food shopping on the way, then stopped to talk to a couple of elderly hikers, a Brit and a German. They told me of a coastal path up to Sunderland that my trailer could probably handle, and some likely camping spots among the dunes at Whitburn, a few miles north of the city. The British fella turned out to be a caravaner (for my American readers: a caravan is a small mobile home people tow behind their cars when they go on vacation. Europe is rife with thousands of caravan parks: it's a particularly European form of glamping) who'd made many trips to Scarborough, where I'm from. I told him of some recent grumblings in the town objecting to motorhomes parking in the foreshore car parks (an astonishingly short-sighted approach to generating income for a holiday resort), and he bowed up like I'd just climbed off his sister. As a caravaner, this guy hated motorhomes with a real passion, and I'd lit the fuse. I grinned internally at the narrow absurdity as I waited out his rant. The audacity of putting a bloody engine in it, eh? Scum of the Earth Bastards indeed.

Sunderland proved to be a far nicer-looking town than its reputation suggests. The population was also a lot more culturally diverse than I anticipated. I didn't expect to see Geordies in turbans, for example. The number of different languages I heard while walking the bike through the city centre was a wonderful advert for integration. I was forced to suppress the idea that travelling the world was a preposterous notion when all one needs do is visit the county of Tyne and Wear, and crossed the River Wear (pronounced 'weir') by the larger of the two adjacent bridges.

I pedalled east along the north bank through the architecturally diverse university campus, modern-looking marina, and buzzing dockland onto the coast, turned left and followed it north.

I stopped to fill up at a Whitburn Bay beach drinking fountain, only to misjudge the pressure and spray the front of my beige shorts in a perfect 'Look Mum, that man's pissed himself' pattern.

One of the more pleasing advantages of cycle touring is one's always leaving. I was never going to see these people again, so I didn't even bother trying to dry out or hide it. Let passersby think what they want. It was really quite liberating.

Whitburn is a former colliery village, once the haunt of Lewis 'Alice in Wonderland' Carroll (there's even a statue of him in the library), sited by low cliffs and a long sandy beach. While navigating another bike path gate at the far end, next to a motorbike cafe, I got talking to a rather rotund, blustery, ex-army public school-type bloke on a fancy-looking electric bike. I asked him if he knew of anywhere suitable to camp, and he mentioned a headland near an old military shooting range which was out of sight and quite scenic. It was reachable by bike, he said, but probably not with my trailer. I silently dismissed his lack of confidence as piffle. The trail was a single track. My trailer was *designed* for single track. We rode on for a bit and chatted. He obviously wasn't from around here, as he lacked the Geordie brogue, and he turned out to be quite the raconteur. I couldn't figure out if he was on cocaine or I'd been slipped an hallucinogenic mickey and it'd animated a British comic strip character from the 1940s. 'Is there a pub anywhere close to where we're going,' I asked, 'maybe one that serves food?'

'Humph, that's a good question, young man, very good question. Now let me think, let me think for a minute. Why yes indeed, there's the Grey Horse Inn, but the last time I went in it was full of yobbos! Mind you, I doubt that'd bother someone like you, what? You look like you could handle a couple of hooligans! Gird your loins and go for a drink, eh? Zip up your glad rags and hit the boozer for a night on the lash? Is that what you're doing tonight?'

I immediately decided I wasn't.

'Yes, they had some yobbos in there a couple of years ago, y'know, fighting and smashing up the place! Scared all the decent folk out, old boy.

Don't know if they cleaned the bugger up yet, but they need to. Can't have bloody yobbos running the place, by God! But I'm sure they wouldn't bother you, though, not with your build, what!'

Sounded like my kind of pub, actually, but I still wasn't going.

He turned off with a wave as the main path angled back towards the road, and I continued on along the clifftop track.

The small headland he'd directed me to goes by the name of Souter Point, and while not quite as spectacular as the headlands I was used to on the North Yorkshire coast, it was extremely pleasant. I pitched my tent as the sun was setting, and watched the light daub the beach and sea with a roiling tempest of oranges, reds and golds. Shit got lovely pretty damned quick.

I finished off the Cumberland sausages with a tin of chicken and vegetable soup, then brewed up some coffee (well, Nescafe 3-in-1 instant coffee with the creamer and sugar cleverly included in a single sachet) and opened a bag of Maltesers while I watched the world power down.

Now, I've had much finer coffee (who hasn't), and much more bling desserts, and I've taken in far grander views, but in that precise moment I'd never experienced a better meal. I wouldn't have changed a thing. I felt an exhausted ecstasy for the first time, the precise reason I'm doing this. A *travelgasm*, if you will. A perfect moment. It was powerful pleasure. Sheer, raw, and unfiltered. Perhaps it was the hallucinogen making a last minute surge, but I'd just discovered my own personal heroin. I could've stayed in that place until the sky fell in, but the sun moves on, and so must I.

Shipwrecks and axework

Leaving my sweet clifftop campsite was like wire brushing a hemorrhoid. The mesmerizing sunrise over the sea compounded my distress. I had to suck it up to press onward, because the promise of Bamburgh castle beckoned, and Scotland dangled beyond. I'd never been to Bamburgh, which is unusual considering my love of medieval history. Bamburgh is one of the more famous strongholds in England, lying on the evocatively named 'Coast and Castles' cycle route, which I was to follow into the lumpy country of uptight religion, boiled offal, and the hair colour I've associated, since a traumatizing childhood experience, with the smell of rotting apple.

I'll withhold names to protect the guilty: the girl who sat in front of me in primary school, with hair like a burst mattress bonfire, had a habit of gnawing apples like a rodent, peeling away the skin first, then the flesh, ever so slowly, while it oxidized. Even at that tender age I couldn't help but internally scream *Jesus Christ, it's turning fucking brown! Eat faster!* but of course, manners brokered silence. One day, immediately after eating her smelly rotten fucking apple, she announced she needed to go to the lavatory, and promptly pissed herself right in front of me. I can remember the smelly rotten apple piss puddle like it was yesterday, spreading on the wooden floor beneath her chair.

Another time, again post nibble, she told the teacher she felt nauseous, and was told to go to the bathroom. Halfway across the classroom she clamped a hand over her mouth and projectile vomited smelly rotten apple stomach mulch through her fingers, all over the front third of the class. Stephen King's *Carrie* had nothing on this lass. I've never seen redheads, or apple sauce, or *The Exorcist*, the same way since.

Years later, while studying psychology at university, I discovered the mechanism of this prejudice, and swiftly moved to eradicate it. It didn't work. Powerful salience, these formative olfactory experiences.

I noticed, down on the beach, a substantial piece of driftwood. It was obviously a ship's timber, and I'd love to have known its tale. One end looked to have been ripped off and a chunk out of the middle was burned away. Oh, there was a story here alright. My imagination, ever eager to exert itself, leaped to compose a yarn of mountainous seas and heroic derring-do as I cycled along the modest cliffs into South Shields.

I've since discovered two Spanish galleons shipwrecked here during a storm while fleeing from the English, following the thwarted Armada invasion in 1588. This timber was most likely a remnant. The locals immediately plundered the wreckage (as you do) and much of the wood was used in the construction of several buildings. One of the ships' bells is apparently still installed at the local church. I don't know about you, but this kind of high adventure stuff makes me giddy as a schoolgirl.

This 26-mile stretch of coast, from the Tees to the Tyne, is one of the most dangerous in the world. There are an average of 44 shipwrecks per mile, blighting the formerly intense maritime traffic in the region. One of the chief culprits is a range of rocks known as *Whitburn Steel*, now warded by Souter lighthouse (the first in the world to be powered by electricity) a mile north of my campsite.

Before the lighthouse was built in 1871, these rocks held the record for a single year, with 20 shipwrecks in 1860. Whitburners must've been rolling in lovely salvage. I'm more than a little surprised the world's first electric lighthouse wasn't smashed with a hammer whenever the weather turned.

I was to meet up with an old friend in Newcastle, but communication issues meant I didn't get hold of him until I was already on the Tyne ferry and committed to a day in the saddle. The perfect weather helped persuade me not to spend the day idling: I wanted to be on the road, and I could always catch him on the way back.

The road through North Shields is characterized by gentrified residential developments in the pervasive dockland fashion. While it looks attractive, one can't help but sense the loss of industry and of Great Britain's ability to make stuff. Throughout history, countries have always relied on heavy industry as their economic backbone, but outsourcing to cheaper countries has obviously changed this dramatically, to what end remains to be seen. The simple fact is when you deflate the industrial heart of a country, you create a massively unemployed underclass. The irony is the people complaining about the hordes of shuffling dole zombies roaming former industrial regions are often the same people profiting from the transition.

The mouth of the Tyne is guarded by the imaginatively named Tynemouth Castle, one of the largest fortified strongholds ever built in England. It's so big it's got its own 7th century priory. This was the home of Tostig Godwinson, Earl of Northumbria and brother to King Harold, and of course, doomed bad guy at the Battle of Stamford Bridge in 1066. By all accounts, the man was a heavy-handed twat, indelicately governing the volatile local blend of Norse and Saxon warlords to the point he was eventually banished by his father, King Edward the Confessor. Part of the problem was he came from a markedly different culture in the south, with a distinctly arrogant method of lordship compared to the more egalitarian north. The North-South Divide existed even then. Indeed, this is probably where it began.

Tostig burned my hometown to the ground in 1066. He and his Grima Wormtongued conspirator, King Harald Hadrada of Norway (who quite honestly deserves a book of his own; Harald was a bad motherfucker in the Conan mould), came ashore with 300 ships at Scarborough on their way to York, seeking allies among the colonial Danes. They were met with defiance, so responded by pushing bonfires down from the clifftops onto the fortified fishing village below, and cutting down anyone trying to escape. (It's worth noting Tostig may have been otherwise motivated: Falsgrave Manor was one of the holdings of his earldom before banishment, then a separate village half a mile inland, now part of Scarborough proper.)

The only thing I knew about Blythe was a lazily browsed TV documentary/reality show about people out on the piss in the town. If the programme is to be believed, the place is packed with blank-eyed twentysomething alcoholics conga-twerking between the gym, tanning bed and dance club. The kind of person, if I accidentally fell into conversation, I couldn't guarantee I wouldn't stab through the heart with a hiking pole. So I deemed it wise to breeze on through, but stopped in at the Morrisons. Feeling adventurous, I gathered the ingredients for a curry, concentrating on the value brands. I bought the cheapest tin I could find of beef madras, along with fresh augmenting vegetables (onion, carrot, garlic, ginger, and chilli pepper).

I dismissed the fear of irradiating my testicles and camped under an electricity pylon just outside of Cambois, breaking out my hatchet *Bumpkinslayer* for the first time, to slaughter some perfectly innocent roots and saplings to make way for my tent. So this is what politics feels like.

Cooking up the curry took a while and I was shocked how much fuel I used in the Trangia. And it was quite mediocre. I'd made curry the same way before, but always with a premium brand, and they turn out much better. Duly noted.

Cambois is a curiously French-sounding name for an English colliery village. The unfounded rumour is it was formerly some kind of French colony. It's pronounced 'Cammus' by the locals, and probably derives from 'camus', which means bend or crook in Gaelic, likely referring to the shape of the bay. 'Cambion' is another Gaelic word, referring to a place of trade or exchange. The portmanteau 'Cambois' began to appear on maps around 1700. Before this it was spelled more phonetically.

Gaelic? I sense Scottish, Irish and Welsh readers gasp, in *England?*! Why yes. These places predate our respective antipathies.

The next day proved why the 'Coast and Castles' route is so named. I had no idea there were so many. I mostly cycled along coastal paths, alternating between remote and tiny villages, broad expanses of sheep-speckled coastal wilderness, and spectacular stone fortresses to remind of Britain's supremely violent (and therefore supremely interesting) past. I passed through Lynemouth and Cresswell, and lingered for a time in the very fetching Amble, with its small marina and port. I stopped for a butcher's at the impressive Warkworth Castle, and while passing through the quaint village below bumped into one of the MG rally guys from a few days ago. He beeped his horn and yelled across the road to me, 'You're going very slowly!' as he drove past. Downhill, I might add. I chastised his combustion-powered wimpery with some unnecessarily obscene body language.

I stopped for the night in an empty field next to a lay-by just outside the very posh Alnmouth, overlooking their expansive golf course. I cooked up some chow mein noodles to accompany a bag of prawn crackers, and got on with *Battlestar Galactica*, which was beginning to come to a head. I was impressed by the multilayered themes being explored, especially the integral links between patriotism, nationalism, and racism. This is the beauty of sci-fi: it can address complex and controversial issues coded in allegory, thereby sailing over the heads of the declawing censors, dumb-it-down advertisers, and offended internet commenters. Whenever someone says they don't like, or get, fantasy and sci-fi, especially after I've pointed them to the good stuff, I can't help but forever label them a fuckwit.

The next day I rose late and was on the road by 9.30am.

I rode ten rough coastal path miles to Craster, having to navigate a frustrating number of hikers' gates, each one specifically designed, it seemed, to make passage with a bike trailer as inconvenient as possible. I was forced to unhook and haul over every time, like a Naval Gun Run for the Increasingly Unmotivated.

In the great scheme of things, these gates don't particularly rankle me that much because I've chosen to travel this way, but in the moment, many sheep, cattle, and elderly ramblers have heard the countryside echo with 'OH COME THE FUCK ON YOU *CUNT*!!'

And while we're on the subject of bike paths, these 'anti-horse' gates certainly don't seem to keep the horses out, and horses shit a hell of a lot more than dogs. We have all these rules in place about picking up dog shit with plastic bags, with special bins dotting pedestrian areas specifically for their disposal, but no one says a word about horse shit. We're talking a volume factor of fifty here, at least. I've mentioned this to more experienced cyclists, and they've dismissed horse shit as the price of cycling bridleways. Apparently it's less sticky and smelly, consisting mostly of grass or hay, so doesn't stick to your tyres so much, and sprays off far less readily. Very important, this, especially when hill-climbing around a corner with your mouth open.

Howick's coastal mesolithic remains are fascinating. Excavated in 2000 and 2002, archaeologists found remains of a 7,800 BC tepee-style hut, which they reconstructed at the time to get a better idea of the process. They also uncovered an early bronze age (around 2,000 BC) cist cemetery containing five stone-lined graves, four of which were sized for infants.

The remains showed their diet consisted of pig and fox, nesting birds, shellfish and hazelnuts. Seal and fish were also likely. The cliffs supplied them with the ever-important flint for tools. At the time, of course, the sea was a couple of hundred yards further out.

Craster, a little further up, is a coastal fishing village allowing only residential traffic, with a large car park for everyone else on the single road in. This seems very theme parkish, but the place is lovely to look at and surprisingly lacking in bouncy castles, obesity, garish carnival lighting and the inbred. Mind you, I was here early in the day so don't take this as gospel. It is a cul-de-sac, after all.

Built on modest volcanic cliffs a mile or so south of the 14th century Dunstanburgh Castle ruins, themselves sited atop iron age remains, the village is famous for its oak-smoked kippers, widely proclaimed as the best in the world.

I bought a cup of tea and sat for a while on a bench overlooking the tiny harbour to bask in the sun and demolish a packet of chocolate digestives. I didn't try the kippers.

I checked in at Dunstanburgh campsite for a couple of days to clean myself up and get some work done. It has a great view of the castle and the staff could not have been more accommodating, allowing me to use their office to recharge all my electronics before I set off again. Alas, I couldn't afford the time to get down to the beach or castle or explore the nearby pub because of a looming 5,000 word deadline. My entire time at the site was spent typing furiously away, stopping only to sleep, eat, shower and do laundry, and they even allowed me to stay well after my check out time to get finished. I can't recommend the place enough.

The Bamburgh conspiracy

My friends and I have an unnamed game, a form of which I'm sure
everyone else in the world plays too, that could be called *Look at this Cunt.*

We're not targeting women, of course, quite the reverse. Working class
men from the British Isles and its derivatives (Australia, New Zealand,
South Africa, etc, but strangely not the closest one, North America) typically
use the word 'cunt' to describe other men, quite often with friendly affection,
or at the very least, minimal malice. North American men seem to have
forgotten this masculine ethic at some point, and get quite temperamental
when so labelled. I think it's got something to do with all the hugging and
constantly talking about each other's 'feelings', whatever those are.

The *Look at this Cunt* game doesn't involve the actual presentation of
female genitalia for inspection, of course; it's more about pointing out an
atypical passerby, perhaps if he's wearing an unusual item of clothing, or
staggering along in an advanced stage of inebriation. Maybe he has a
nervous tick, or a limp. My current favourite is the Justin Bieber haircut,
which to me looks like a toddler's licked a Walnut Whip and dropped it at the
barber's.

Now imagine, if you will, a man cycling through a British city centre
towing a single-wheeled trailer, dressed in clothing so loud it diverts
shipping, topped by a helmet not unlike the bell end of a penis. This image
opens *Look at this Cunt* season with finger food, fireworks and a free DVD.

So I figured, over this first week or two of the bike tour, my lifetime
cunter/cuntee aggregate had swung heavily into the negative. This kind of
imbalance is, obviously, not very zen at all. I needed to redress the cosmic

equilibrium somehow, so I decided the best course of action would be to find people even stranger than me to have a good bloody gawp at.

I considered attending soccer matches for a while, because you've got to be pretty weird to enjoy that shit when there's perfectly legitimate sports like rugby and mixed martial arts available instead. Any 'sport' that requires its participants to avoid physical contact isn't real competition, let's be brutally honest here, it's calisthenics. Sport was conceived to supersede war, not knitting. And as for the fan segregation, well, that's definitely worth watching, if only for the immensely entertaining 'HOLD ME BACK, LADS!' dynamic. But football games cost money to attend. Which brings us neatly to libraries.

Libraries positively brim with weirdos. I've never been the coolest guy in the building, but if the reading rooms in every town I'd visited so far were any indication, I'm Elvis bloody Presley. Children and pensioners are exempt from the comparison, of course, but the middle ground is filled with characters you wouldn't trust with either.

Libraries also have the dual advantage of being somewhere you can plug in to charge up and log on. There are vast discrepancies between local governments' attitudes towards these two things, however. Some bend over backwards to accommodate their library visitors' needs, while others hoard their electricity and internet access like they're their own private precious. These grasping, shrivelled, Gollum-like authorities put their employees in a very uncomfortable position when someone like me comes along, who isn't above questioning such reticence. After all, charging even my full suite of electronics and backup batteries works out at around a penny. I'd happily bung them the money to cover it, even 2p. Often these employees would lie to me rather than simply explain their county council employers were so inarguably, stunningly, frustratingly stupid. I had one say the wiring in the building was so old plugging my laptop in would blow the lot. I don't know if I was more miffed by not being able to charge up or that I look so dumb I might buy such absolute horseshit.

I figured out through trial and error that my interaction with the person behind the library counter goes a long way to determine their subsequent helpfulness. If I was monosyllabic while I joined up for the day, there was often a poorly disguised suspicion of vagrancy. However, if I chattily revealed I was a writer, it was like The King himself had swaggered in wearing the cape outfit and a cocked eyebrow, sporting an expectant semi.

There'll be more on this later.

I left Dunstanburgh campsite at 3pm after writing 5,000 words of inane corporate drivel for a client who requires that sort of thing, and rode a meandering ten miles to Seahouses, a small holiday resort on the expansive Northumbrian coast. I passed a touring French couple coming the other way who'd been in the British Isles for three months, zigzagging north through Ireland and Scotland, now heading south through England.

I felt a real kinship with them, even though we only chatted for a few minutes. Not because of the cycling, but because of the travel. It's the shared pace of it, I think, and the attitude of going wherever and doing whatever you want. Proper freedom.

I bumped into another cyclist on the outskirts, a local heading to the shops, who joined me for the ride through the town, and gave me advice on things to see and places to go. I stopped to use an ATM and nose around a bit, then hit the beachside road to Bamburgh with the idea of finding somewhere among the dunes to camp. 'No Camping' signs galvanized my determination, but I couldn't find anywhere appropriately accessible and secluded. I eventually gave up, puckering a bit as darkness began to descend with a few drops of rain, and decided to high tail it through Bamburgh and see if I could find somewhere suitable further inland.

It was dark by the time I did, and the rain was steadying. By the light of my headlamp I pushed down an overgrown farm track and found a flat bit as it cornered into a ploughed field. I quickly threw up the tent and got under cover, but fell prey to the beginnings of the deluge.

I packed up at first light and realized I could see the iconic castle from my campsite. Not too shabby.

I headed back into Bamburgh to find somewhere to work, preferably with a good mobile data signal. I found one, surprisingly enough, on a bench atop a sand dune overlooking the castle, and badged as one of the ten top lunch spots in the UK. It even had a little plaque. I dare say no one in the UK that day worked from a grander office.

I spent a few hours proofreading and polished the work from the last couple of days and sent it in, then whiled away the rest of the day looking around the village. I visited the church and the Grace Darling museum, did a little food shopping, then headed up to the castle to check on what time it opened the next day so I needn't limit my exploration. I discovered it was a tenner to get in. A fucking *tenner*?!

Outraged, I stormed back down into the village for the Castle Inn and spent twenty quid on beer to calm myself down. My more liquid perspective determined this may be the only time I ever visit Bamburgh, and this is a castle I've been fascinated by my entire life. I decided to have dinner in the pub, too, and ordered a ten quid burger. (Is everything a tenner around here?) What should have been a pricey gourmet extravaganza turned out to be a commercial patty and oven chips, though the salad was acceptable. For a tenner, it should come with a back rub and a fucking blow job.

Feeling exploited and a little annoyed at myself for falling for a tourist trap trick, I concluded I should go to the castle tomorrow morning, and left the pub to camp in the same place as the previous night, falling asleep to the final episode of *Battlestar Galactica*.

First thing the next day I went to refill my water bottles from the sink in the public toilets, only to notice a sign I hadn't noticed the day before:

NOT TO BE USED AS DRINKING WATER

I'd thought the two litres I drank yesterday tasted a little off, but figured it was my imagination. My stomach plopped, just once, in agreement. Better get this castle seen before the squits kick in, I reasoned. I took a precautionary dump and dashed off on a whirlwind tour.

I managed to cruise all the major sights before sloppily machine-gunning a commode in the castle toilets for an hour. While so engaged, I fired up the GPS, plotted an optimal route, and during the first brief armistice in the bombardment, made a break for the nearest pub that wasn't the tenner-for-a-TV-dinner Castle Inn.

The Victoria Hotel is the other proper pub in the village; there is a third, The Mizen Head, but it's more of a fancy restaurant. I ordered a pot of tea and a reasonably priced egg salad sandwich, broke out the laptop, and made the first of a good dozen visits to the lavatory over the next five hours. To cut down the frequency and avoid bloodying my arsehole with repeated wiping, I held the gravy at bay as long as possible. I'd relent when my bowels began to cramp and groan like an old wooden ship. The bonus effect of these longer intervals was the population of the pub would turn over, so no one saw me make multiple trips except the bar staff, and they weren't really paying attention. I'm not sure why this concerned me.

I'm fairly sure the tap water in the public toilets had been messed with. Why would it not be connected to the mains when the building is bang in the middle of the village? It's likely the sign was placed there to encourage bottled water trade with local merchants, and the tap water smelled like disinfectant, which suggests an easy way to taint a water supply is by tossing a urinal soap cake into the water tank.

I'm not being cheap by avoiding bottled water, but when you average 4-5 litres on a regular day, never mind a hot or hard one, the cost becomes prohibitive, and you require regularly spaced shops. Thus my water filter. It will process chemically affected water, but I need to know to use it in the first place, and the counterintuitive sign placement had caught me out. It was set far above the eyeline, probably to prevent kids tearing it down.

Still, there was a sign, so it was ultimately my own fault.

Unconnected to my rectal regret, I was disappointed by the castle. Not that it isn't a fantastic structure: the problem is people still live there. Residents upgrade interiors over time, so the current decor bares little aspect of the original, and it's the original I'm interested in. In a lot of ways, I'd prefer a ruin, because my imagination can more readily fill in the blanks.

I want to experience how the medieval warlord lived, not the Victorian or Edwardian gentleman, though those periods can be similarly fascinating, y'know, if you're a stiff-necked ponce obsessed with restriction. The final straw was the exit through the recreated torture scene in the unconvincing dungeon that led into the (admittedly nicely-stocked) gift shop. I think it may be a sign of advancing age that I stopped to browse the treacle fudge despite my digestive urgency. On the whole, however, my Bamburgh visit taught me a valuable and shrewd lesson: don't pay to go in castles unless they're ruined.

All I do is eat and shit

It seems to me the word 'adventure' is sorely misused. Simple travelling could hardly be thought of as adventurous, despite the insistence of the more insular among us. Unless we're fording raging jungle rivers to the accompaniment of distant cannibal drums, or at the very least while shitfaced, I think we should refrain from such pretentious ennoblement. The majority of Facebook photo albums I've seen with the word 'adventure' in the title seem to involve little more than its advocate gawping at the camera, holding a pint.

If this is what passes for adventure, I'm Doc fucking Savage. Nevertheless, it is true that alcohol infuses enterprise with exploit. This is its purpose, after all. Thus, it could be said drunk people are society's foremost adventurers, because they face jeopardy in the most mundane of deeds: negotiating a kerb, for example, or unlocking their front door, or whipping up a snack without setting fire to the kitchen. Additionally, drunk decision-making is notoriously perilous, and adventure, by definition, should involve risk. Columbus, Cabot, Magellan and Cook were teetotallers all[1], forced to ridiculous lengths to find similarly stout adversity, so they don't impress me any more than a drunk does, and shouldn't you. Now, if they'd been sailing into those tropical cyclones on their third bottles of sherry...

Many of the most exciting times in my life involved alcohol. For example, I've woken up in cities I didn't start out in with women I don't know, who've bizarrely introduced me to their children over breakfast. Or

[1]I made this bit up.

during one particularly memorable morning, a husband. He gave me a ride to work. And then there's the one about the brothelkeeper's daughters. But these are stories for a different day.

The biggest problem with inebriation is forgetting stuff, so a lot of adventures, or rather the hugely-entertaining lessons of injurious *mis*adventures, often go to waste. Luckily, the colossal advantage we have nowadays is camera phones. Now we can record events to remind ourselves in the mornings, and if we forget to push the button, someone else invariably pushes theirs. Technology is bringing light to the dark corners of our memories, reminding us to embrace the things we'd rather forget. We're starting to weave much healthier 'warts and all' narratives. Attempting to dismiss a difficult episode from our consciousness is to forgo the benefit to our personalities. Hardship breeds character and perspective, no matter how it's induced.

Before you steeple your fingers in condescending concern; life, I firmly believe, is about the acquisition of anecdotes. When the battery on my mobile runs out, I've often sat back by the campfire to contemplate the things I've done and seen, and sweet Jesus, has it been fun. I chuckle myself to sleep like a loon. Now, there still exists those in society who frown on enjoyment and hold austerity dear. They espouse hard work but consider 'work' sitting at a desk. These people are dying off, thankfully, as automation and outsourcing shifts our western focus from industry to entertainment. After all, we only get one life; we may as well whoop it up.

It's no coincidence that religion preaches such drab virtues: work hard and create lots more workers. Keep quiet. Don't think. Do as we say. The powerful and parasitic love these teachings, which is obviously why they nurture them. They need workers to keep working, after all. And what better motivator than the threat of damning their eternal souls? It's the biggest scam in human history. One has to step back, as George Carlin said, in fucking awe. The enormous, outrageous gall of these people beggars belief. It's only over the last few years I've begun to realise the magnitude of the deception. I was a worker ant for a long time, but, since turning professional with this writing malarkey four years ago I've had a lot more space to read, observe, and think, time-dependent luxuries rarely afforded us working class scum. This blinkered veil, thickened by decades, nay, generations of rudimentary, incessant, infectious social propaganda, is lifting.

And will, no doubt, reveal some real adventure.

I decamped and backtracked into Bamburgh for breakfast. A cracking little delicatessen called The Pantry caught my eye, so I went in for a cup of tea and delicious handmade turkey and coleslaw sandwich. This tiny place is much more than a sandwich shop, though: the shelves were crowded with local artisanal produce, including the first beef jerky I'd seen in the UK. A couple of decades in Texas has made me a huge fan of the stuff, but I wasn't sure how well it would suit a fruit pastille-popping cyclist, and it'd be an expensive experiment. I repaired to a nearby park bench to eat, then went back in for another cuppa and a cheese and onion flan, famished after yesterday's gastro-intestinal hostilities. I wish I'd tried this place rather than the Castle Inn.

I chatted with Julie the owner, herself a budding writer, for a while over yet another cup of tea and some local fudge. She'd been in Bamburgh thirty years, obviously loved the place, and said she was determined to write a memoir about it. She displayed the common reticence of the unpublished, unfortunately, which could be considered a very British trait; I experienced it myself back in my embryonic days of inflicting inflated amorphic drivel on the unsuspecting public. I gave her as much encouragement as I could while cautiously attending any menacing churns or glops stomachward.

I bought half a pound of back bacon from R. Carter and Son's butchers a few doors up (*Est.* 1887. I seem to have adopted the innocent Yank-like wonder for such prestigious longevity) and hit the road north.

Even after my hobbit-like first, second and third breakfasts I was feeling very drained and tired. So much so when it started raining around midday I fucked this shit, set up camp in a roadside forest, and was deep into the first season of *Arrested Development* when *Bowel Hell II: Revenge of the Quiche* held its first guerrilla screening. After a trouble free morning, I'd thought the bug gone, but it wasn't. It'd been lurking, bibbed-up, cutlery poised, waiting for a meal.

The next sixteen hours were spent howling liquid brown destruction into a hastily dug hole. I spent so much time squatting outside the tent I set up a tarp shelter to divert what little rain breached the natural forest canopy, primarily to keep my Nexus 7 dry so I could continue enjoying the tribulations of the Bluth family while crouched to my berserking toilet. Shitting into a bag in a tent is all unicorns and lollipops when it's only once every day or two, but this kind of persistent onslaught calls for infrastructure.

Depleted to a point where the beast in my belly could but growl and belch malignant whiffs, I pushed on for Holy Island. I stopped for supplies at a service station on the A1 crossing point, but found it so ridiculously overpriced I didn't buy anything, and went to the nearby Lindisfarne Inn instead for lunch and to do a bit of work. I ordered two sides instead of a main: chips and onion rings. Hand made, generously portioned, perfectly cooked, and quite possibly the best onion rings I've ever had. What a refreshing, non-grasping, astute attempt to acquire, keep, and grow a reputation by delivering excellence rather than a Bamburgh Castle Inn wallet raping. I washed down the delicious repast with three pints of ice cold Carlsberg, and headed coastward to the *Barn at the Beal* campsite in glorious sunshine, burping happily.

I camped down next to a couple from Newcastle who'd driven up with their mountain bikes for the weekend. They'd brought not just a tent, but tables, chairs, a three ring gas stove, crockery, cutlery, you name it. That evening I felt very underequipped breaking out my backpacking Trangia to fry up some bacon, pan size necessitating a single rasher at a time. I silently resolved to buy a bigger set; judging by the uneventful elapsed time since lunch, the stomach bug seemed to have relented.

The *Barn at the Beal* is probably the best campsite I stayed at the whole trip; in truth, it's more a destination than a campsite, the latter an addendum to the facility. It's essentially a hugely popular bar/restaurant/coffee shop that acts like a nightclub/pub on Saturday nights, and it was Saturday. But I had to work, and the view from my tent across the causeway to the Holy Island of Lindisfarne was stirring enough to hold my attention. This was the home of St. Aidan and St. Cuthbert, where the Viking age began in Britain, with Norsemen coming ashore to raid the isolated monastery on the island in 793 AD.

I took a break from work and rode the mile down to take a look at the famous causeway, which was hidden by the tide. I checked the posted times and figured I could cross in the morning, and cycled back to the site, my front tyre picking up a huge thorn twig on the way. I literally had to stop and pry the bastard loose. And here's the curious bit: an hour or two after getting back to camp the tyre was flat. In the daylight next morning I pulled the wheel off to fix the flat, but couldn't find an obvious puncture. I went to the bathroom, filled up the sink, inflated the tube and rotated it through the water. Not a bubble. What the hell? I put it back on the bike, pumped it up, and it didn't go flat again until the next puncture about five weeks later. EXPLAIN *THAT*, SCIENCE!

Judging by the noise that night, the *Barn at the Beal* knows how to party down. I resisted the temptation to join them, knowing full well if I did, no work would get done tomorrow, and quite possibly the day after, and I had deadlines.

The next day I cycled the couple of miles over the causeway on a gloriously unloaded bike to Lindisfarne, and very nice it was too, though very touristy, even mid-October. I wanted to check out the church, but it was Sunday morning and religious people were gathering for a preachin', so I made myself scarce before they could capture me and turn me into their anal fuck gimp, or whatever it is the devotional do in there.

I wandered through the priory to discover there was precious little left of the 8th century buildings. The existing ruins are the remains of the 11th century replacement. Shit. Still, they're impressive, and for someone who's spent the vast majority of his life in construction, intriguing. It was built to mimic the appearance of Durham Cathedral, some 80 miles to the south, where the remains of the legendary St. Cuthbert, Prior of Lindisfarne from 685 to 687AD, are now interred. St. Cuthbert was such a popular saint he became perhaps the most important in the British Isles, spawning a huge cult and remained incredibly influential until the Protestant Reformation a thousand years later. Interestingly, the Lindisfarne Gospels, an exquisitely illuminated bible written in honour of Cuthbert shortly after his death in 687AD, was the first to contain elements of Celtic, Anglo-Saxon, and Romanesque art and stylings, using inks and dyes from as far afield as the Himalayas. It was perhaps the first step—a catalyst, if you will—into bringing the fractious and unruly pagans of the islands to the Catholic heel. This is where Christianity first blossomed in the English-speaking world (or rather the geography of it, as English didn't exist yet). Even so, it was surprisingly exciting to simply be in the vicinity of such extraordinarily pivotal history.

I rode up to the castle but didn't go in, because I'm not fond of paying to be disappointed, then rode back to the campsite for bacon sandwiches and a mug of tea.

It was a beautiful day, so I had the tent wide open for the view, and found if I laid down using my backpack as a pillow, with my knees propped up, feet wedged against the tub groundsheet wall to prevent them sliding away, I could rest my laptop against my thighs and write with Lindisfarne as a backdrop. *Travelgasm* number two.

That's right, I seem to have stumbled upon the most momentous discovery in the history of literature: writing lying down. I'd just made the easiest job in the world even easier. This is the kind of innovative laziness I bring to the table.

By midafternoon, I decided it was time for a break from the doing of nothing, and figured I'd head up to the coffee shop for something sticky and sweet. Plus I had that morning's shitbag in my tent's redundant second foyer to dispose of, so I'd chuck that in a bin on the way.

Unfortunately, as I rounded the corner of an obscuring hedge, I bumped into a whole herd of elderly hikers standing around their cars chatting, and me carrying a translucent bag of shit. I had my laptop in my other hand, so quickly put the offending article in the same hand in an unsuccessful effort to shield it from their view. I faltered a step, and considered turning back, but my inner monologue piped up BRAZEN IT OUT, MAN, BRAZEN IT OUT! THEY'LL THINK IT'S OLD FOOD OR SOMETHING, WELL IT IS, IN A SENSE. This forced me to stifle an involuntary laugh, which emerged as a loud staccato snort, and drew everybody's attention. This in turn, of course, gave me the giggles.

I viciously clamped them down. Straining purple, veins popping like a power-lifter, I strode stiffly to the rubbish bin, struggled for an awkward eon to get the lid off, and discovered it was full. But of course.

Time slowed to a smear as I weighed up my options. By now, they'd figured out I was carrying a bag of shit. This was the only bin between the campsite and the coffee shop. At a loss for alternatives, I gently placed the bag on top of the trash, and carefully replaced the lid so as not to burst the bag. 'Bloody dogs,' I said.

I was really in the mood for a scone with jam and cream, but they had already run out, which is testament to the popularity of the place. I went with a fudge slice and a pot of tea, and outstanding it was, too.

Work, work, work

Travel is fatal to prejudice, bigotry, and narrow-mindedness, and many of our people need it sorely on their accounts. Broad, wholesome, charitable views of men and things cannot be acquired by vegetating in one little corner of the earth all one's lifetime. - *Mark Twain*

I rolled into Berwick-upon-Tweed (population 13,000) and, as usual when entering a town after days in the country, had to stop myself from talking to people. Berwick has the strange geography of actually being further north in England than a substantial portion of Scotland, which is truly unusual. Almost as unusual as the guy who stopped for a chat on the 17th century bridge. He was a backpacking RAF helicopter pilot, attached to a search and rescue squadron, which incidentally is the same line of bullshit I used to run on girls to get in their pants when I was in my late teens. I don't recall it ever working, but I do remember scamming along with a mate playing the RAF pilot I'd 'rescued'. On our first go, while well beyond the opening salvo with a couple of attractive prospects down the pub, their friend returned from the bathroom and said 'Hi Stef.' We'd both gone to school with her, so that was the end of that. The perils of trying to pull gash in the small town one grew up in.

So I initially regarded this fella with deep suspicion. However, his bay window accent credentialled his story, and he was setting off on a multi-day hike to Alnwick, which is just the kind of boring crap people with real accomplishments do.

Berwick is an interesting place. It changed hands between England and Scotland so many times when we fought over such things, it achieved a uniquely independent status, almost as a separate state, so much so official proclamations used to refer to '*England, Scotland, and Berwick-Upon-Tweed*. One such document was the declaration of war against Russia in 1853, and signed so by Queen Victoria. At the treaty of Paris in 1856, mention of Berwick was unfortunately overlooked, so the town remained at war with Russia for the next century. It wasn't until 1966 when the London correspondent of the Russian newspaper *Pravda* paid a visit to officially put an end to hostilities. The mayor of Berwick at the time, a playful wag named Robert Knox, told the Russian to 'Please tell the Russian people through your newspaper that they can sleep peacefully in their beds.' Which is all kinds of awesome. This is the genial currency missing from current international politics. But then, real war does tend to sour the charm of political flippancy.

I had a look around the shops in the town centre, bought some meths (denatured alcohol) for my stove from a decorating store, and found a central bench to sit on and people-watch for a bit. Dole enthusiasts and pensioners dominated the scene, as they typically do in the middle of a weekday when everyone else is at work. The former can be fun to watch, because the threat of violence typically simmers just below the surface. This is especially true of the tattooed womenfolk, who seem to think loitering behind a double-barreled pushchair while nursing a heady morning cocktail of smartphone, cigarette and their latest black eye the de rigueur accoutrements of social status.

I left Berwick by the way of Aldi and Morrisons to get some food in—Morrisons was rapidly becoming my favourite supermarket in Britain:

they seem to have the best prices for quality nosh and they make lattice-topped pork pies with cheese and pickle baked in, which I'd quite merrily stab a dole baby for.

I hit the border, one hilly section of the road actually *being* the border. I stopped to take a self-timed photograph by the WELCOME TO SCOTLAND sign, with the intent of making it look like I was urinating on it, but it didn't turn out well: I looked like I was fiddling with something way smaller than it actually is. Plus, it didn't say WELCOME TO SCOTLAND, it said WELCOME TO THE SCOTTISH BORDERS, dramatically disarming the irreverence. I resolved to do a better job when I found the proper sign, but I never did. (I was planning to do the same thing to any WELCOME TO signs I saw, so rest easy, Scottish folk.)

I hit my first mountain in Scotland, and it was a doozy. I didn't make it all the way up pedalling, but I took a healthy chunk out of the bastard and impressed myself with how fit I was getting. It took me two hours to get to the top, factoring in water breaks and occasional collapses of exhaustion. I later found it was only a 200 metre hill, around 650 feet, but I could've sworn it was bigger. I stopped at a cattle and sheep farm on the top where the farmer graciously refilled my water bottles. He was 70 years old, and had lived at the same farm since he was three, and told me the winters were often a bitch up here on his hill. I was forced to correct him with *mountain.*

I hurled myself down the descent and covered the two-and-a-half miles to Ayton in about seven minutes. Two hours up, seven minutes down. Now we're cooking. To celebrate my first major downhill I bought an eight pack of Carlsberg to wash down the ham salad sandwiches I made for dinner, but only drank three before passing out to the first episode of *Fringe.*

I gave a good yank on a stubborn tent peg this morning and it flew out of the ground and off into the woods, never to be seen again. I also couldn't find my phone after packing. After much searching and retracing of steps it turned up as a lump in my sleeping bag compression sack. Little bastard.

I considered *Fringe* as I repacked, and wasn't sure if I liked it or not. Seems to be the *X-Files* with even more dubious science, and decided to be offended by the insult.

I spent the day in the busy fishing port of Eyemouth after using their post office to send home a few redundant pieces of kit: a pair of shorts (it was getting cooler), a rugby shirt, my unused collapsible water carrier, my large laptop (the battery life is so short it may as well be a brick), and the mosquito head net now the midges had died off. An elderly South African couple owned the branch, after moving here to be nearer their daughter living in Edinburgh. 'Close, but not too close,' was how they put it, knowing full well their offspring's propensity for offloading grandchildren.

I invested in some treacle toffees from the proper sweet shop across the street, replete with jars of candy lining the shelves, measured loose into a paper bag by hand. Ah, nostalgia. Then I spent the rest of the day in the *The Tavern* attempting to work but largely staring out of the window at the scenic rocky bay. At one point a stray dog got trapped on some rocks as the tide came in, which was far more interesting than whatever it was I was supposed to be doing. It took a good while to realize there was no owner coming to the rescue, and everyone else around was well into their pension years. Shit, looks like I'm getting wet, I thought, and started packing up my computers to go rescue the daft bloody dog. Just as I'd got everything nicely logged off, closed down, cables rolled, packed up, and halfway out the door, he took the plunge himself and swam ashore. Cursing canines the world over, I went back inside to set up again.

I left in the late afternoon and climbed out of Eyemouth's coastal dip, battled a howling headwind along the tops until I found a sheltered spot to pitch my tent in the valley made by the scandalously misnamed River Ale. A couple of friendly coppers stopped by for a chat to make sure I wasn't a serial killer, and left clutching business cards, promising to read my blog. Ahh, the old Abrutat charm.

I camped for a day to rest up, then struck out for Dunbar, the birthplace of famous Scottish explorer and American busybody John Muir. I'd never read any of Muir's stuff, indeed, I'd never heard of the fella, but as the token transatlantic diplomat I am, I felt I should, and barrelled through his house, now a museum, on the way to the pub. Interesting guy, this Muir. He was born in 1838 and emigrated to a farm in Wisconsin with his family in 1849 (which is now a National Historical Landmark). After some schooling he wandered to Canada to avoid the civil war draft, and settled in Indianapolis thereafter. He made money by working at a wagon wheel factory, where an industrial accident left him blinded for six weeks. Confined to a darkened room to aid in his treatment, his entire philosophy changed. Much like going on a bike tour, I'm sure he found himself in the position of actually being able to think about things, at length, for the first time in his life. On recovery he walked 1,000 miles from Indiana to Florida, indulging his passions for the wilderness and botany. There he worked in a sawmill for a bit, then became a sailor, and ended up in California living in a remote cabin and writing about his studies of geology and botany. There his legend was made as an advocate for the Sierra Nevada Mountains and western forests, especially Yosemite, and thence nature in general. I felt lesser for not having read him, so I put him on the list and, hungry as a horse, I hot-footed to a hostelry.

My pub of choice was the Castle Hotel, where I had an affordable lunch of delicious homemade steak and ale pie with real chips and peas that'd shame the staff of the namesake Castle Inn in Bamburgh to slow and hopefully painful suicide. The friendly landlord's name was Gordon Collin, who used to own a pub in my home town of Scarborough, and we counted a few of the same people among our friends. Small world, indeed.

I left the pub at 6pm. Boosted by half-a-dozen pints of lager, I was confident I'd find somewhere amenable to camp, but didn't. The sun was well set by the time I discovered a quiet field corner by the bike track, threw down my tent in a huff at the delay and woke the next morning with the promise of Edinburgh.

If you know the way broadly, you will see it in all things. - *Miyamoto Musashi*

I've always been impressed by people who could blow their nose without using a handkerchief. Whenever I'd tried it myself I looked like I'd lost a sinus fight with a snot monster. Unfortunately, I'd forgotten to bring a hankie on tour, which necessitated an acute learning curve. I started out stopping by the roadside to gingerly pinch each nostril shut in turn while bending double to avoid snotting my shoes and trousers. The noises I produced were not unlike a barnyard during the pig rut, punctuated by much wiping and lots of *shit*s and *oh, for fuck's sake*s. I was wonderfully pathetic.

After a couple of months, however, I was blowing my nose with the poise of a professional footballer. I didn't need to stop pedalling or even pinch, just a casual flick of the head and a silent snort sent a brace of mercurial missiles flashing into the periphery, scattering my DNA across the planet to further complicate the question of where I'm from.

It's a joke of some lineage among my American friends that I don't adhere to any particular cultural group. I was born in Canada, raised in the UK, with a German father and an English mother. I went to university in Wales, and lived for 20 years in America. This confuses the hell out of your average Yank, who thinks everybody should be easily identifiable for shooting, bombing, and/or imprisonment purposes.

I'd become an expert judge of wind and trajectory, instantaneously triangulating with relative velocity. I could womp rat storm drains like a trainee Jedi, using my philosophical training to quell the urban Dark Side urge to decorate any dole enthusiast loitering too close to the kerb.

If I did need to nip a nostril on a particularly gushy day, I fired the right one under the left nipping arm, followed by the left one over the top after dropping the elbow and rolling the wrist, switching from right to left nostril with a thumb to middle finger move and a slight turn of the head, in a seamless Legolas-like combo that's frankly deserving of at least a video game franchise.

So I was quite pleased with my personal development.

A man on foot, or horseback, or on a bicycle will see more, feel more, enjoy more in one mile than the motorized tourists can in a hundred miles. - *Edward Abbey*

One of the great pleasures of travelling this way is entering a small village completely unaware of its history, and leaving thoroughly entranced. It's these between places that motorized transport denies us.

I'd never even heard of East Linton (population 1,800) in East Lothian, a small village with an impressive global legacy. It's home to the modest

Preston Mill, dating back to 1599, still in operation, and open to the public, although I didn't go in because of the hefty entrance fee, and my wallet was still weeping in the shower after Bamburgh.

I'd had some fun with ancient mills already, too, but this place was where millwright and engineer Andrew Meikle grew up and worked, and the man was a legitimate lightning bolt. He invented spring sails for windmills in 1772: wooden slats that opened and closed to control the rotation no matter how strong the wind, which revolutionised the milling industry in a time when a mill was by far the most important building in any community. He also invented the threshing machine: since the beginning of agriculture, harvested grain had to be threshed from the stalks and husks by hand, usually with large flails. Meikle's invention automated this extremely labour-intensive drudgery. In one perfect swoop, he reduced annual agricultural labour needs by 25%. Y'know, for the entire world.

Obviously, this didn't make him very popular with farm workers, who rioted in 1830 as threshing machine proliferation, along with the Enclosure Acts, began to seriously hamper their livelihoods, At this time in history, the loss of livelihood usually meant the loss of *life*, not comfort, like it does today. The Swing Riots, as they became known, were intended to destroy threshing machines and protect farm workers jobs; the only directly-linked death was one rioter, probably at the hands of a farmer or soldiers. The end results, however, were nine rioters hanged, and 450 sent to Australia. Serves them right, bloody technophobic ingrates.

Meikle's work inspired a young farmer's lad in the village, who would spend all his spare time in the millwright's workshop, fascinated by the wealth of complexity and innovation. John Rennie grew up, and after a spell at the University of Edinburgh, seemingly single-handedly designed and built every bridge, dock, and canal in the UK, as well as the breakwater at Plymouth Sound, London and Waterloo Bridges, London, East India, and West India Docks, to name but a ridiculously insignificant fraction, and all by the time he died at 60. He was laid to rest with great ceremony in St. Paul's Cathedral in 1821. He only outlived his mentor Meikle by ten years, who died at the venerable age of 92, who is buried in East Linton near his beloved mill.

Quick note about lifespans here: The incredibly high historical infant mortality rate skewed the average lifespan statistic heavily downward. After countless thousands of hours reading history, archaeology and anthropology texts, mountains of studies and acres of research reviews, I discovered that, back when muck was a condiment, if folks made it out of infancy they often lived well into their seventies and occasionally beyond. Even in pre-agricultural societies (including those still around today) the average adult age at death was around 54. And this was in a very sharp and pointy world before sterilization, safety rails, and interfering cunts with clipboards. So the idea we were teetering by the time we were 30 is rather naïve.

I ascended a valleyside on a very pleasant single lane road, paralleling the River Tyne (yep, there are two, this Scottish one's a little more modest) and rode along the tops. The sun came out to brighten the world and made me chuckle at the audacity of the views. There really is nowhere on Earth quite as fetching as the British Isles on a sunny day. It's in a class all its own, like cycling into the lid of a giant shortbread tin.

I came upon Hailes Castle, a *proper* castle, in ruins and with little evidence of Victorian tampering. There was no entrance fee, gift shop, or indeed another soul in sight, just a big ruin in the middle of nowhere and little ol' me. Now we're talking. I spent an hour wandering around, imagination clicking into overdrive, empathizing with the sheer effort involved in the building of such a thing, and the battles fought over it. I pictured the place intact, with rendered walls, whitewashed, in the medieval style, with slaked lime solution to prevent erosion. Castles weren't the great stony edifices we see today, they were smooth and bright white, the whitewash reacting with carbon dioxide in the air to form a hard chalk surface. I lingered in the vaulted basement kitchen and could almost hear the clang of pots and pans and the shouting at underlings while a lord's feast was prepared. At some point in the castle's working life a new, larger donjon had been built, and the old keep converted into a massive dovecote for the keeping of pigeons, which were an important source of eggs, meat and dung during the medieval period.

In 1400, Hailes Castle successfully withstood an attack by a force led by Sir Henry 'Hotspur' Percy, a warrior of great renown from the very Warkworth Castle I visited in northern England, and so named by the Scots for his ferocity in battle. He had a career as a solider and diplomat that sent him all over Europe, as far afield as Cyprus, before he rebelled against Henry IV of England and was killed at the Battle of Shrewsbury in 1403. His body was exhumed after its first burial, beheaded, quartered, and sent to the four corners of the Kingdom to counter rumours of his survival, before being delivered to and buried by his widow at York Minster, forty minutes from my home, in a tomb I've passed on countless occasions. Hotspur achieved immortality as a character in Shakespeare's *Henry IV, Part 1*, of course.

Oh, I had a whale of a time.

Haddington (population 9,000), the next town along, is one of those places that just stays with you. Drenched in the morning sun it's an absolute beauty. The bike path came in over the 17th century Nungate Bridge, surrounded by the parkland of the medieval St. Mary's Collegiate Church. I stopped for several minutes in the middle of the bridge just for a bask.

The longest (rather than the largest) church in Scotland is really of cathedral scale, which belies Haddington's current size. In the middle ages, however, Haddington was the fourth largest town in Scotland, and has seen some serious history, being burned down numerous times by Scottish and English armies alike.

I found the excellent library and spent the afternoon working, then left by way of the riverside bridleway, narrowly avoiding smacking the crap out of two older teenagers as I turned to follow the river. I can't even remember what they said, but their aggressive tone forced my ego to skid to a stop.

They had a couple of girls in tow, so they tried playing hard men and both postured up. I wordlessly ditched my backpack and was actually walking towards them removing my helmet before reality gripped, and they fled. I think the cold grin did them in.

Not sure what I would've done had I decided to chase them down with my re-emerging cardio. Something crippling that doesn't leave a mark, probably. They treated me to offensive gestures as they backpedalled, so I returned the favour, dipping into my exponentially more appalling construction lexicon. They had no answer, so I considered it a moral if hollow victory as I climbed back on the bike.

Am I going to do this every time someone takes the piss? I decided right there and then not to. From now on I'll just give them a wave and a smile, or uncurl a middle finger. Peace, young padawan. No need to break someone's legs for being a smart mouth. You were similarly objectionable once.

Soothed by this newfound life structure, I stopped at a Co-op and bought a tin of Heinz Baked Beans with Hot Dogs for dinner because I hadn't had them since I was a kid and why the hell not. I also picked up a bottle of white wine and a half priced tin of Devon custard, a steal at 47p, and I like custard so much I'm quite happy to eat it like a big yogurt.

As darkness drew near I happened upon a little picnic spot by the track, slightly elevated above a small car park and screened from the trail by trees. I got my tent up and thoroughly enjoyed the beans and hot dogs with some bread and butter, which got me very nostalgic about my time in the boy scouts. I watched the movie *Super 8* as I ate to compliment the experience.

I got my head down early, but was woken at 11pm by the sound of souped up ricers congregating in the parking lot below. I'd forgotten it was Saturday night. I've never been one to complain about the noise of partying, lord knows a hypocrisy on that scale could fracture the firmament and annihilate the entire physical plane of existence. But they couldn't see me from where they were, so I lay awake and eavesdropped on what conversation I could filter from the dental equipment-like whine of their tiny motors. (If you're going to buy a car, kids, buy a goddamn CAR, for the love of all that's combustion powered.) They talked about diminutive pistons and micro gears and wee exhausts, some of the most boring shit I'd ever had the misfortune of overhearing. After a couple of surreal hours I was longing to open up a vein with my Swiss Army Knife, but would've settled for a cloak of invisibility and a sack of root vegetables. Or even better, a Molotov Cocktail.

I'd just started contemplating the empty wine bottle, an oily bike chain rag and a half-litre of methylated spirits when they wisely buggered off. Finally alone, I slipped into sleep and woke to a dew-drenched morning. I packed up and quickly fixed an overnight flat, then hit the trail into

Edinburgh, possibly my favourite city in Europe.

It was spitting rain as I rolled around the base of Arthur's Seat into my familiar Scottish stomping grounds. I'd been up to Edinburgh maybe eight or nine times in my early years before I moved to America, so I passed a few pubs I remembered falling out of, streets I'd streaked down, and parkland I'd pissed on and passed out in. The nostalgia washed over me in rich golden waves. It's curious we have such affection for chaos. Or maybe it's just me. Edinburgh is my favourite because it's probably the finest city to get drunk in on the planet. The civic buildings are magnificent, the Edwardian and Georgian architecture a real joy to meander through, and the pubs were built by men who knew precisely what they were doing: evenly spaced, and individually unique. No chain pub nonsense here, where one interior looks much like another. At least, not in my experience, as I didn't actually go in any pubs, but made a beeline for the MacDonald library, the only one open on a Sunday (as far as I could determine with a spotty data connection). Riding through the crowded Sunday lunchtime streets reminded me of London. Edinburgh had changed. And there were hipsters everywhere, which I'd thought was a purely American thing.

What's a hipster? A hipster is a youth clothing and behavioural trend, given to retro fashions and, as far as I can tell, the overt dismissal of anything approaching a work ethic. You're not going to find a hipster down a coal mine, for example, or pouring concrete, or tiling a roof. They seem to work and congregate in coffee and sandwich shops, claiming to be artisans and artists, apparently a product of affluence and the internet. Also, your average hipster tends to vehemently deny being one, like homosexuals in the fifties.

The particular hipster working the reception in the MacDonald Library,

South African if I can place an accent, looked at me as if I was stuck to the sole of his hemp loafer. I announced my wish to join for the day so I could use their WiFi. 'Why not go to a coffee shop?' he volunteered contrarily.

I didn't reply 'Because it's none of your fucking business, shithead. Close your mouth and punch the card before I drag you out of here by that ridiculous steampunk moustache and smash it through your head on the kerb outside,' because that would be alarming for the poor boy and I'd be straying from my newfound philosophy of peace. I'm sure he was simply attempting a little human interaction, he just wasn't very good at it. He worked in a library, after all, and he was a hipster.

The reason I didn't go to coffee shops much is because they're prohibitively expensive. I'd do so if there's no other option, but when a coffee costs as much as a day's food, it's difficult to justify buying five or six to accompany a day's work. Similarly with pubs, though a pint can last a good while longer than a coffee, even though I'd developed a taste for cold coffee while living in warmer climates.

The library shut at five. I made a run for the outskirts to find a place to camp, trying to beat both the rain and the dark and failing miserably on both counts, getting lost several times on the way. I cheered my predicament considerably with a visit to a Morrisons, where I bought bean sprouts, shallots and some soy sauce for a stir fry with Thai noodles and prawn crackers. Finally around seven I found a flat bit of grass and pitched, but the topsoil was at best an inch thick so I had to get inventive with the guy ropes and weight distribution inside: thank Christ I bought a free standing tent.

Suits, robes and uniforms

The light of morning showed I'd pitched directly next to a copse of woods with a far superior site in the middle. Shame, because I wanted to lounge around for a day and work. I decided I was too lazy to break camp for the trivial reason of relocating only thirty feet, so I packed up and set off for South Queensferry instead, the southern terminus of the famous Forth Railway Bridge with a library open all afternoon from one until eight.

The onward cycle path ran through a palatial country estate of ancient woodland, manicured lawns, rocky coast, and the occasional posh person out walking the requisite black labrador. It's strange how our stereotyping processes whir madly to life from the merest hint of plum in a cheery 'morning'.

The path turned to follow the coast, and brought the Forth Railway Bridge into sight, the first time in my life I'd ever seen it. I had to stop pedalling with the enormity of it all. It really hit home, at that point, how much of the island I'm from I hadn't seen, and this icon was only a couple of hundred miles from where I grew up.

How can anybody possibly have an opinion about their own country, or any other, for that matter, when they haven't even seen the thing? Our opinions on everything we haven't personally witnessed are derived third hand from media, not actual interaction. I suddenly realized I didn't know a fraction of what I thought I did, and the idea was both depressing and elating at the same time. I was depressed because I knew had a lot of work to do, but elated because, as far as work goes, this is about as fun as it gets.

Completed in 1890, the Firth of Forth Bridge was built under the watchful eye of the world after the collapse of the Tay Bridge during the winter gales of 1879, where 75 people perished when their train pitched into the estuary. Renowned for their excellence in engineering the empire over, this shook the Scots to spare no expense and build a bridge that would never fall down. The Forth Railway Bridge was the result.

The cantilever design over the Forth river is one of the strongest and most expensive ever conceived, the latter quality being why there are so few like it. The unfortunate irony is 98 men died building the thing.

At the time, and for 27 years, 1,710 feet was the longest single cantilever span in the world (there are two of this length on the Forth Bridge). It is still second only to the 1,800 feet of the Quebec Bridge in Canada.

Ingredients

- 54,000 tons of steel
- 194,000 cubic yards of granite, stone, and concrete
- 21,000 tons of cement
- 7,000,000 rivets

Now, we may build larger structures today, but in the 1880s they had no combustion power. So when you sit and look at this colossus as I did for a couple of hours, and factor in a dash of construction knowledge, it makes one feel comparatively useless and unmotivated. Luckily, these are traits with which I'm intimately familiar.

I scouted that night's campsite under the road bridge a mile or so westward and put some work in at the library. The meticulously attired Indian librarian opening the door treated me with overt contempt. Overt enough to annoy me, at least, and I'm pretty difficult to irritate. He queried my possession of a library card (this library fell under the Edinburgh umbrella so my membership from the day before was still good), then he said there was no WiFi, when my phone told me there was. I didn't cause a fuss because I needed to work here, but what an absolute twat. I didn't let on I was a writer, as our interaction was already soured by his shitty attitude and I didn't care to engage him further. I hoped he was going to be working the day after, so I could plan to come in muddy booted or after eating something particularly gaseous. That'd sort him out.

I left at eight o'dark, rolled by the supermarket to pick up some leafy vegetables (good for wind generation), camped down and had a stir fry again, but for some reason the improvised concoction didn't taste quite as spectacular as the night before, probably due to the inclusion of so much cabbage, eggs and beans. I only ate half and chucked the rest. I spent the remainder of the night finishing off the third season of *Mad Men*, and was truly impressed by the amount of shagging going on. It's well-produced porn with discreetly obscured genitalia, let's be honest.

The next day I was straight back to the library. The attendant this time was a woman, so I dutifully wiped the fresh mud off my boots outside before going in, and chose a spot far from foot traffic so my uncontrollable farting wouldn't bother anybody. What a waste of a biochemical stockpile. My distain for the dude yesterday doubled with each apocalyptic release.

I finished up at around 4.30pm and crossed the Forth Road Bridge to look for a camping spot on the north bank. It must be over a mile long, and has some cracking views of the rail bridge.

I tried to make it through Dunfermline onto a trail where I could camp, but darkness caught me on the nearside outskirts. At a loss, I pootled around until I found a patch of woodland in a business park, not perfect but good enough. I planned to be up early for a dash to Stirling before the forecast rain arrived anyway, so it was as good as anywhere else.

The route to Stirling followed another railway track converted into a bridleway, which I've found to be the quickest way to get somewhere on a bike without riding on the main roads. I rechecked the weather on my phone before I left, and it looked like I had a little more time than I thought, so I made up a flask of tea and some peanut butter and jam sandwiches for later.

I bombed along the track to Stirling, covering the twenty miles or so in only a couple of hours, and lost my two litre water bottle on the way. That's four I'd lost. I'd been tucking them into the front of the trailer wedged between my backpack and the pivot arm post, but for whatever reason they kept becoming dislodged, despite several differing attempts at tying them in place with a bungee. I had to rethink this, because dehydration was starting to get old. I decided on putting the new bottle in the same place but wrapped in a plastic bag and tying the handles to the top of the post so if it did slip from position it wouldn't be sacrificed to the thirsty road gods.

I sought out the Stirling Central Library and emailed a normally reliable client about a delinquent payment, and checked the Doppler weather radar. Rain was imminent, so I had to make a run for the hills to find a campsite. My plan was to never cycle in the rain unless I absolutely had to, and I had a few miles to go yet, so I didn't wait for a reply and got moving.

Potential camping sites on the way were thin in the ground, and the sky started to spit, but I eventually found a likely spot in the shadow of an uprooted tree by the golf course in Dunblane. I got set up just in time before the heavens opened, and settled down to tea, PB&J sarnies and *Mad Mating* season four.

When I ride these long and relatively boring stretches (old railway lines tend to have little in the way of views) I get to think a lot. Probably more than any other time in my life, actually. The freedom allows one's mind to roam like an illiterate Italian. Let's ignore, for the moment, whether such musing is good, indifferent, or a portent of gathering doom. Currently, I'm toying with the notion of the world being nothing more than a giant LARP game, and I've become increasingly convinced this might actually be true. (Live Action Role-Playing is a popular kind of improvised interactive theatre game, where people get dressed up as elves and gnomes and whatnot to act their way through (typically) *Dungeons & Dragons*-type scenarios (you can see examples in movies like Role Models and the award-winning documentary *Darkon.*) It may well be a scenario worth considering anyway, true or not, as it's a beautiful bypass of the conditioned social hierarchy our 'authorities' so carefully bludgeon into us, and one I seem to be slowly jettisoning.

My subversive reasoning is the people who purposely dress in the daftest costumes (clerics, police, military, politicians, business suits etc) are the ones who seem to disappear into their roles the most, and forget, or never even begin, to function like normal members of an integrated society: egalitarian, peaceful, stress-free, kind, and bemused by the ridiculousness of it all. Let's call it 'enlightenment', or the baseline human condition. They're the true neckbeards, the socially inept goofballs who don't possess the ability to function outside the construct of the game, never get laid properly, and carry their puffed delusions of authority like a favourite lightning bolt beanbag. The more I thought about it, the more it amused me. And I started to feel sorry for them, and realized I was turning into a hippie.

Google 'hunter-gatherer societies', our natural and default state. They exhibit all the previously mentioned mutually beneficial tendencies far more readily than we of the current industrial habitat. Any graph you'll find plots immediate-return hunter-gatherer communities at, by far, the happiest. Agrarian societies are the most miserable, and our Western industrial-digital paradigm lies somewhere in between.

Also consider 'necessity breeds invention'—probably the most accurate maxim ever to describe progress—Paleolithic technology didn't change much for many hundreds of thousands of years until some bright but lazy spark invented agriculture, which tells me 'necessity' was sorely lacking. The popular idea among archaeologists is populations probably grew to a point where agriculture eventually became necessary, hence its advent 10,000 years or so ago, but for many hundreds of thousands of years before then we were running around killing and eating organisms like we'd evolved to, happy as pigs in shit. Now we outsource such tasks, technology advances exponentially, stress is our biggest killer, and according to the Mayo Clinic, almost 70% of us are on prescribed antibiotics, opioids, and antidepressants.

Recent arguments with inflated local politicians, and soldiers freshly returned from furthering wealthy corporate interests in the Middle East, who insist the West should eradicate the entire Islamic wing of religion, almost a quarter of the world's population, because, and I'm paraphrasing only slightly here, they're *Lawful Evil*, have been the catalyst of this LARP idea.

For those who don't know what the hell I'm talking about: When E. Gary Gygax was writing the first rules to *Dungeons & Dragons*, he wanted to introduce a simple method to define a character's motivations, so he invented *alignment*. Initially, this consisted of three primary morality systems: *Chaotic*, *Neutral*, and *Lawful*, each of which were later subdivided into *Good*, *Neutral*, and *Evil*, for a total of nine separate subcategories. Simplistic, but really quite clever. Choosing one gave the player an immediate behavioural framework to explore, and the Game Master an idea of how consistently the character was being played. The *Lawful Evil* alignment is typified by a deep belief in the structure of law, but will exploit that lawfulness to hurt people. Many extremists fall into this category, like the Westboro Baptist Church. For *Lawful Neutral*, think a by-the-numbers courtroom judge. The *Lawful Good*, on the other hand, temper their belief in law with altruism. Nelson Mandela springs to mind as an example. Actually, he's probably more *Neutral Good*, or even *Chaotic Good*, because he fought against the laws of South Africa in his early years. Maybe he changed to *Lawful Good* over time?

Anyway, the soldiers seemed to base their opinions on their experiences with the backward Afghan hillbillies they were fighting (who are obviously no more a representative demographic of Islam than our own outlying twitchy meth-head rednecks are of Christianity), coupled with the propaganda I'm sure is foisted upon them to keep their motivation elevated during the conflict. Many pointed to genocidal urgings in the *Quran* during our arguments (which tells me they're likely parroting the same 'approved' leaflets), neatly sidestepping similar themes in the *Bible*, and claimed their 'uniforms' were not 'costumes' (tricky things, labels), and guns aren't substitutes for foam rubber LARP swords at all and how fucking dare I?

Intelligence is often described as the ability to abstract: usually characterized by the willingness to consider more than one opinion on the same subject. If this is lacking, especially for purposes of intellectual growth and amusement, one should probably refrain from engaging in conversation on anything more meaningful than, I dunno, NASCAR, on pain of me vigorously stabbing at one's carotid artery with a fistful of pub darts.

So how do we drag these lost LARPing fools back to reality? I alone can't explain the depth of their subservient folly to each individual cog in the establishment machine. That'd take millennia and I don't have a time warp spell memorized. What we need is some pervasive mass media approach, like a book.

Oh.

Thinking and wilting

With all this dangerous and subversive thinking I've been doing on the bike, I've managed to formulate several trains of thought I later discovered to be established philosophical paradigms, often dating back to the Greeks. So my ego deflates at my unoriginality, but at least I'm in good company.

Apparently I'm a *hedono-anarcho-primito-apocaloptimist* if I string everything together, which broadly means I like the kind of freedom that kicks permission in the nuts, simple but elegant comforts, and plan to thoroughly enjoy watching society implode when the technological singularity grips society in a few decades. Bye-bye Dickensian hierarchy, hello inherent egalitarianism. (I've probably misspelled these prefixes, and may indeed have made a couple up, but who really gives a shit about Latin outside ivory towers and Harry Potter fans?)

Now, some people might think this just another political rant, but I'm talking about a much larger perspective than socialism versus capitalism, here. Technology is catalyzing such a colossal change in western culture we're entering completely unexplored territory. (Socialism doesn't work, it is said, because a few members of society will always be capitalists (our societies are too large and unintegrated for the social repercussions of selfishness to be effective), while capitalism requires secrecy and cunty behaviour to operate, an inevitable perpetual transparency will force both to go away.)

I think we're reverting to behaving the way we've most evolved to behave, and our drift back to the village is the first step towards this more communal living. Think about it, we've spent perhaps 400 generations as property-owning agriculturalists, but the previous *hundreds of thousands* of generations lived in small, social, largely self-sufficient groups. With which lifestyle do you think we're more comfortable?

Technology increases access to information, and the powers that be typically derive their influence from controlling that access, so the two are constantly at odds. The powerful want to keep us regular folk arguing among ourselves, not questioning every move our extorted tax dollars make. Unfortunately for them, technology is growing exponentially from a global wellspring, and people all over the world can now communicate instantaneously, for free, despite myriad efforts to stem the flow. The fractious natures of the world's governments and their sponsoring corporations are their own stumbling blocks. This selfish grasping mentality I've been going on about, works to their disadvantage. Which is sweet justice indeed.

See, when technology and biology finally and meaningfully merge (if the overwhelming consensus of futurists' predictions hold true), we'll be actually able to sense each other's thoughts, or true moods at the very least. Deception will become a thing of the past. As dark as this will probably be, I imagine we'll rapidly familiarize with the novelty, and models of acceptable behaviour will revert to previous village-like integration, finally sloughing the crippling shadow of strict Victorian influence. (It was the Victorians who popularized the restrictive, repressive social etiquette, with which we're all still familiar, throughout the Western World. It hamstrung our social development for generations.) And this time we won't have some rat-faced inbred lording over us playing peasant Wack-A-Mole.

I'm looking forward to a sober reassessment of the antisocial ideas of property, race and organized religion that've been cluttering culture since we started planting crops. I've often wondered at the universal ridiculousness of one bit of the biosphere claiming to own another, and inexorably come to the conclusion that property = violence. Without violence, property is meaningless, even when we dress the wolf in the sheep's clothing of legislation and a police force.

Of course, I would've discovered this far sooner if I read more philosophy books, but there aren't enough explosions, car chases, or lusty sluttish women to be found amongst the pedantry, as far as I'm concerned. And I've been too spoiled by the likes of Terry Pratchett and Douglas Adams to wade through dusty pages of rhetoric without the promise of at least a chuckle to lure me on.

If more of us valued food and cheer and song above hoarded gold, it would be a merrier world. - *J.R.R. Tolkien*

After three and a half weeks on the road, I decided it was time to go on The Big Piss. I mapped some pubs and a route, and after securely locking my bike and trailer in camp, I headed off on foot for a hostelry engagingly titled *The Tappit Hen*, located in the shadow of Dunblane's grandiosely labelled 'cathedral', which is really just a sizeable church.

The liquid personalities were all less than £3 a pint, however, which dared me to try at least one of each and more of those I liked, and there were six available.

A few happy hours later I swayed exuberantly out of the *Hen* and meandered to the *Riverside*, cheerily acknowledging every passerby with a lurid wink or conspiratorial gesture on the way. My inexplicable favourite became the discrete index finger nose rub of *The Sting* fame. I'm not even sure what it means, but it feels like we're sharing a secret, which is always fun.

The *Riverside* was more of a fancy restaurant than a pub, and I felt rather out of place sitting at the bar while Dunblane's suitably attired waltzed in for dinner. I delved into a menu, alerted like a sniffer dog to the Gallic semen word *aioli*, downed my pint and lurched heroically over the bridge to the *Village Inn*. This was far more my scene.

I got talking to a few construction lads sitting at the bar. I can't say I miss the hardship of the decades I spent in such work, but I do miss the banter of men who measure their day in sweat, blood and bruises. There's a purity to physical professions that infuses their opinion with authority, a purity that can't be matched by those who get paid to sit in the air-conditioning, myself now included. Making friends quickly, we downgraded to the slightly grubbier *Dunblane Hotel* over the road, and spent the rest of the evening solving global problems. I do vaguely remember quizzing everyone in the bar about their opinions on Scottish devolution, hopefully with my trousers on, which they wholeheartedly dismissed as a stupid idea. In fact, during my entire time in Scotland I didn't find a single supporter of the movement, which I didn't expect at all. Mind you, I didn't ask as many people as I perhaps should've.

Drunk-hungry at kicking out time, the fish 'n' chip shop (that also bizarrely sold cigarettes) across the road was shut; however, one of the lads told me of an exceptional Indian restaurant up the hill, so I said my goodbyes and wobbled up the incline on legs no longer familiar with this level of inebriation.

I decided quite quickly that the *India Gate Tandoori* was far too nice for the likes of me and ordered to go, with a pint while I waited. Curry in a tent on a golf course? I mused, leaning heavily against the bar and feeling a Tom Jones song coming on, first time for everything.

Now, you know the popular marketing idea that people don't remember what you say, but how you made them feel? The same seems to be true with late night curries. I don't recall what I ordered, but back in the tent I experienced some kind of gastronomic rapture. Damn, it was good. I woke up the next morning wearing it like a balaclava, but damn, it was good.

The next day was all rain. Ambitions for the road dashed, I fired up season five of *Mad Men*. I did need some food, however, so after a couple of episodes I made a run for Tesco. On the way, a window cleaner, obviously far more capable than I after our night in the *Dunblane Hotel*, grinned at my dishevelled appearance and bid me a hearty good morning.
This little connection struck me immediately, despite my delicate condition. The humanity in it. I'd made friends in a foreign *town*, not out in the countryside, where such interactions are more expected. The ritual of the pub seems to subvert the 'stranger' barrier. I couldn't for the life of me remember his face or what we talked about the night before, but it gave me a little glow of community I didn't know I'd been missing. British pubs are good for that; they typically serve as the living room of the neighbourhood. Bars elsewhere seldom fulfill the same role.

My goal was sausages, and the result was more sausages. I bought so many sausages in my befuddling hangover I created an instant oligarchy of Scottish sausage barons and established Dunblane as the new Offal Capital of the World. Not content with clearing the supermarket shelves, I staggered under the massive weight of my meaty purchases to a local artisan butcher's shop, whose window pies had been rioting for my attention the previous couple of days. I ordered a warm chicken and ham, and while I was disappointed at the use of a microwave the butcher introduced me to my first truly impenetrable Scottish accent.

It was a granite surge of consonants. I'm fairly used to Scottish accents having grown up in an English town with a high percentage of retirees from north of the border. So, I managed to decipher the occasional 'big man', which I took to be a compliment, but the rest could easily have been coded attempts at homosexual grooming, or suggestions for what meat products I might prefer addressing rectally. I nodded neutrally and said 'absolutely' and 'indeed' whenever a gap appeared in the staccato. I like to think the universe's hidden camera will ultimately cut to the lonely incoherent butcher grimly masturbating by an empty public toilet glory hole and percussively barking 'fukkin' cocktease!' in subtitles after an appropriately comedic pause.

Back in the tent, I cooked up some links with peppers and onions and finished off season five of *Mad Fucks*. I loaded up the first few episodes of *Deadwood* for a change more than anything else, but again, like when it first came out, I couldn't get into it after the first couple.

The next day was a Saturday, and my electronics needed recharging after the last few days of laziness. I hiked to Dunblane library, but weekend hours eventually steered me towards a coffee shop. How expensive can it be? I reasoned, in my hangover's hangover. It was ten quid for two cups of tea, a croissant and a scone. So this is how the Scots were able to give up plundering.

Disillusioned, I went back to the tent and started on season six of *Mad Tits*. I did do a quick run to the cigarette/chip shop at 8pm, just to see if fish 'n' chips away from the northeast coast of Yorkshire continued to be lesser fare. They do, but they were cheap and filling, and that was good enough.

I was going to set off this morning but the forecast rain dissuaded me. The window of time to find an appropriately secluded campsite in Callander would be too small, I reasoned, if the rain stopped at noon and I set off then. And I needed to buy some waterproof pants and gaiters, but nowhere in Dunblane, as far as Google was concerned, were such things sold at a reasonable price.

I decided to leave the next morning, Monday, so I could stop by the library for recharging and still have time to see Doune Castle of *Monty Python's Holy Grail* and *Game of Thrones*' Winterfell fame.

I pulled up to the junction leading off to the castle, and a burly road worker (by appearance, at least), blocked the way with a 'road closed' sign. I asked him if I could still get through with a bicycle, as most road works leave a channel for pedestrians. He said 'no', and refused to elaborate. Usually construction lads with such jobs are glad of a chance to chat: not this dude. Strange. After further tight-lipped answers, I figured they must be filming *GoT* today, and reconsidered the importance of television in general. In hindsight, I should've made up a bullshit story of travelling the world by bicycle visiting Python sites or some other such nonsense, and got him to engage the production company via walkie-talkie. Might've worked. I couldn't care a fig for the stars of the production, you understand: though I love the show, I just wanted to see the castle. I'm a big castle man, if you haven't figured this out yet.

On the way to Callander library for work and recharging, I scoped out a camping spot in the woods on the way. I arrived an hour or so before they closed for lunch. During the enforced break I walked to the main street and brunched on five custard doughnuts and a cup of tea, and memorable they were, too. Thereafter I visited an outdoors shop to buy some waterproof trousers, and baulked at the £22 price tag. So I bought some silicon spray instead, determining to spray my regular trousers and render them waterproof. Like that was ever going to work.

The library closed at five. Rain relocated me to the nearest pub, one *Crags Hotel*, and I spent the vast majority of my time bullshitting with the locals rather than getting any work done. Still, I managed to get pretty lubricated, and waiting for the rain to ease seemed to increase its intensity. By 11pm, it was *fuck this shit* o'clock.

The place I'd selected to camp was off the bicycle track coming in to Callander, elevated off the path (people tend to look down elevations rather than up) and hidden by a bank and some trees. However, I was drunk and got lost several times. It was only while trying to wrestle my rig through several inches of mud in a pitch black farmer's field a good mile from the nearest street light I realized I needed to start being more systematic about my navigation. I propped the bike up, covered myself with the bike poncho, and fired up the GPS.

On a positive note, I did invent a few new swearing combos. On a negative note, my dedicated sleeping bag drybag isn't. There is nothing worse than going to bed wet and cold. Scratch that. Yes there is: waking up wet and cold, knowing you have to change into colder wet clothing. The next morning I grimaced and did it anyway, packed up, and hit the road hard to generate some warmth.

Deery me

The howling tempest blew my fifteen stones completely over twice, and fellow climbers with slighter frames were forced to either crawl or turn back.

The storm began to rage at about three thousand feet, a horizontal arctic blizzard painfully sandblasting any exposed skin. I didn't have my sunglasses with me, so I was forced to march leaning forty-five degrees forward with my head bowed in the classic mountaineering pose, digging for purchase with my one good hiking pole (the other had seized up in the telescopically retracted position) and feeling very Captain Oates. Temperatures plummeted into the negative teens. So this is why people are always dying on Ben Nevis, I mused, stepping around more sensible souls setting up emergency bivouacs. With visibility down to less than twenty feet and snow violently ripping across the rocks to drift waist-deep in blasted leeward pockets, wandering from the obscured path and over a cliff became a real possibility. And I'd waited a week in Fort William for good weather.

I'd arrived at the town, nestled in a valley at the foot of the mountain, wet and knackered after two days of determined cycling over exhausting highland roads. I'd made this mad dash through Glencoe from Callender because an old rugby mate I hadn't seen for twenty years was passing through on his way to a family holiday on Knoydart, a remote peninsula to the north, and we'd arranged to meet for a pint. I rode ninety miles in two days, hauling half my weight again, over mountains, in the rain. For a pint. I want to make sure everyone understands this bit.

Of course, it was to see James Brickell too, and meet his lovely family. Of course it was. I'm not an animal.

Even so, I hold that the first pint of ice cold beer after a hefty day of physical work to be one of the true wonders of humanity's agricultural endeavour. You can keep your cups of tea, coffee, Mexican Cokes, Pinot Noirs or flutes of Champagne. It doesn't even have to be good beer, just lager at the point of freezing. To me, it will always sound the end note to a hellish day, a sluice of civilization scything through the choking dust and murderous heat of Texan summers, and the first bell of sitting back with good company, suspending the dread of tomorrow's forever Dantean descent. That first draught evokes all the firsts I've quaffed before, compounding the refreshment with thoughts of tougher days. It's the realization of an American beer advert. And I figured, after *two* days of sweaty and aching unpleasantness, that first pint might just be twice as good.

I'd modified my route while camping on the edge of Loch Venachar, southwest of Callender, a more dreamlike location I couldn't easily imagine. I had the entire lake to myself, and spent the broad evening hours reclining against an ancient oak, gazing over rippling quicksilver, tracing the alpine crags beyond the far shore as they blushed with fiery streaks of pink and crimson, pondering humanity and our place in the Universe. Well, I would've, if I hadn't inexplicably developed the liquid shits again and spent the entirety of this potential poetry pageant crouching behind a bush, dismayed by my rapidly dwindling toilet paper supply, and personifying a far less elegant but likely more accurate summation of the human condition.

I really should switch to leaves, but fear the experimentation with unknown species. What if I inadvertently wipe with something toxic or abrasive? These grim details are the vital hints survival manuals and TV programmes curiously neglect. Ray Mears never seems to ask his wizened native shamans about this particular topic, you'll note. One can cope with an heroic dose of hardship while one's unmentionables remain dry, unchafed and lesion-free, but introduce something as innocuous as a paper cut to a strategic location and the romance drains from a wilderness journey like dignity after a vindaloo.

The next day I waited for the rain to stop, which it did around noon, decamped and hit the road. I stopped to do a quick smalls laundry in a highland brook and quickly realized I was washing my underpants in water enterprising Scots bottle and ship to the world's wealthy and gullible, and felt quite devilishly ennobled.

I managed fifteen miles that afternoon through the most incredible scenery I'd seen yet, passing a grand total of five people after Callander, and rode past Loch Lubnaig. I took a peek at the very lovely Loch Voil the next morning where the bike route hairpinned around its valley, then switchbacked up the mountain by Lochearnhead. On the way I stopped at Strathyre's *The Inn Bistro* for refreshment and a recharge after my wallet took another arse pounding at the village general store. You know it's in for a raping when you see multipack soda cans shamelessly displaying their NOT TO BE SOLD SEPARATELY labels from the shelves. They could at least have the decency to Anne Frank them in the fridge, for crying out loud, that way the larceny comes as a nasty surprise at the end rather than a gathering dread. More ardent stereotypers might blame the Scottish predilection for frugality, but the owner was a cockney who'd moved north of the border, no doubt, to join in the merciless fleecing of wide-eyed tourists.

As darkness fell I found a likely campsite in a deserted parking area high in Glencoe. I was startled to discover a huge highland stag standing at the edge, about the size of a pony but powerfully built and with a full set of antlers. He seemed less surprised than I was. Like a typical townie twat, I cooed at my luck in happening upon such an elusive creature, and gingerly pulled out my camera for a shot in the fading light, wary about startling him. Strangely, though, as I slowly approached, the animal didn't move, but stared at me. I found this a bit unnerving, as I considered myself much more of a threat that he obviously seemed to, and his headgear began to look a little more ominous than a hat rack. After a minute or two I made a sudden movement to test his moxie, careful to keep my rig between us. He huffed once and nonchalantly sauntered off rather than fled in a panic. What kind of 'shy and elusive' behaviour is this shit, Attenborough?

I found a flat area of grass off the hard standing and put my tent up, somewhat troubled by the encounter. As soon as I was situated I found I actually had a good data signal despite my remote location, and got on the Google. Turns out red deer rut in October and November. It was late October. Great. He was either going to kill me or shag me. Should make for a lively night.

I got some dinner down me and hit the hay, allowing the mating calls of the other stags scattered about their territories across the plateau to lull me to sleep.

The beast returned during the night, however, and began patrolling his own domain, bellowing his location to the hinds. He seemed to be staying away from the tent, which is a good thing. I found the situation faintly ludicrous, and therefore perfectly worthy of comment on Facebook, as I wasn't going back to sleep anytime soon. My transatlantic friends, still awake with the time difference, of course, found the deadly situation highly entertaining, and sympathy was thin on the ground. Even James Brickell, or 'Bricks' as we call him, the university rugby friend I was to meet in Fort William, and now a noted natural history documentarian, dismissed the peril as naivety on my part and marvelled at my luck at having an interactive opportunity with a five hundred pound feral hormone fuck monster twenty miles from the nearest hospital.

I pictured antlers suddenly plunging through the tent walls above my head, and decided to prepare. *When Animals Attack* videos are the limit of my experience with fang and claw combat. I figured Romeo had a headful of handles, so one option would be to get my mitts on those to prevent it stabbing or slashing me, getting behind them and twisting its head round like a rodeo cowpoke wrestling a steer. Then I remembered deer also kick with their front legs, so instead I might need to keep him at bay with something to allow a good strike with the hatchet. Hiking pole! I got one out and telescoped it to its maximum length. If he charged with his antlers I could fend him off before dropping the weapons to grab and twist him to the ground.

This presented an entirely new set of problems, though. Can you armbar a deer? Triangle choke? Hardly. Sod that, then, stay on the feet, keep him at bay and hit him in the head or neck with the hatchet, that would be the best option. Thus formulated my plan. I'd need my headlamp on to see what the hell was going on, too. And wear my shoes rather than my slip on camp sandals: secure footing is important in any fight.

Turns out the beast was disinterested to say the least, as he stayed away and I eventually drifted off. At 3 am, however, he let out an almighty moo literally inches from my sleeping head. *He was right beside the tent*! I spasmed three feet into the air with a falsetto shriek, while swaddled perfectly horizontal in my mummy sleeping bag. I hung for a Michael Jordan moment, reality slowed to a smear, before bullet time recalibrated and I crumpled back to earth. My embarrassment at the sound I'd made coupled with the short-sighted fug of the rudely awakened stirred me to violence. I struggled out of my sleeping bag and started digging for my hatchet and shoes, roaring with fake bravado, 'IF I HAVE TO GET OUT OF THIS FUCKING TENT....!!'

I heard him move away, sniggering like Muttley. He didn't return, and I, of course, couldn't return to sleep. I spent the rest of the night fully clothed and headlamped, senses scrambling to every imagined sound, improvised weaponry at the ready. I've never been so grateful to see the sun come up.

The ten miles of mostly downhill to Glencoe had to be one of the treats of the tour, despite the rain, which, to be honest, never really got going until I turned northeast towards Fort William. I draped on my US Army poncho, which is great for keeping the rain off your top half but does trap the heat when you're working hard, so I ended up drenched in sweat anyway. I got into town about midafternoon and Google mapped a bike trail around the estuary, which I followed until I found a remote camping spot. I managed to get the tent up without saturating everything else, ate two tomato sandwiches and the rest of the quite ordinary but prohibitively expensive toffee cake I'd bought from the cockney criminal mastermind in Strathyre.

I got a text from Bricks to say he had arrived at the nearby *Premier Inn*, and was sitting down to dinner in the attached *Brewer's Fayre* restaurant. I biked down in the rain and spent an entertaining evening meeting his family and parents, who were polite enough not to mention my unkempt appearance and smelling like a rugby changing room, while Bricks and I had some fun catching up on twenty years apart, desperately trying to curtail our swearing. It turns out he wasn't the tea boy on the children's natural history show *Deadly 60* at all, or even a production assistant, but the actual head honcho.

So the BAFTA it had won was, in fact, on his mantelpiece at home.

Suitably impressed that someone I've seen drunk and naked more times than I care to remember had actually amounted to something, I went for a piss and caught sight of myself in the mirror for the first time in a few weeks. I looked like a caveman from a fifties movie. Hair sprouted from each ear like a cliffside alfalfa crop and a glistening thicket of nose hair tumbled into my mustache. I'd dropped significant weight, too, but as I was somewhat rotund when I set off, this was no bad thing. I shoved the nose hair home with an index finger, wiped myself down as best I could and returned to the table, apologizing for the horrific sight I was inflicting on everyone. They graciously pooh-poohed my apologies and shoved another drink in my hand. Awesome company.

I woke around eight, and had a hangover lie-in with a couple of episodes of HBO's *Rome*. Casually Google mapping, I realised I should be able to see Ben Nevis from my campsite, so I rolled out of my pit and lo, there it was.

It had been obscured by the rain yesterday. I decided I had to climb it, but only when the saddle sores had at least begun to fade. I checked the weather and Tuesday looked promising. I tidied myself up with a little grooming, haunted by the image in the mirror from last night.

I rode into town for the library. There was no WiFi and only one thirty minute computer slot per day was allowed, but I was permitted to plug in, which was at least something, I suppose. I left at one o'clock and shopped at the extremely busy Morrisons for some cheese, bread, tomatoes, and a couple of tins of ravioli. They had no Jamaica ginger cake, curse the heavens. I decided to try and use my new bank debit card. I'd just opened my first British bank account a couple of months earlier, and was woefully behind on this chip and pin technology lark, but I had to learn sometime. At the self-service checkout, I stared intently at the unit for several silent minutes but couldn't find anything approximating a credit card slot. With nothing obvious and a crowd gathering, I began wiggling the card into every crevice on the machine in a process of elimination, occasionally turning to shrug at my audience, rolling my eyes at the growing gulf between a spiralling society of technophiles and the prosaic wisdom of the common man. Fortunately, the woman came over and saved me. She said I was the best one yet.

Back at the tent I cooked up the last of some hot dogs with fried onions and ketchup, just about one of my favourite food combinations in the world, and when the rain broke I erected a washing line and hung out the wet gear from yesterday, and set up the candle heaters to dry my boots.

The next few days were spent alternating between the tent and the library, occasionally visiting a pub for the WiFi. Despite timing my runs back and forth, I invariably got caught by the rain at least once a day, so my attempts at drying out became futile. The estuary began to flood, too, especially at high tide, and the footbridges in the parkland I was camping in disappeared under several inches of water.

One particular time in the library, two librarians were organizing books where one of my batteries was plugged into a wall socket. The elder one, obviously in charge, a stooped Miss Jones from Rising Damp lookalike, with rounded shoulders, a pot belly, and hair dyed so black Picard would send in a probe, admonished me, saying we were only supposed to charge the device we're working on. A demonstration of her supreme authority to her underling, no doubt.

Weary, by now, of this jobsworth nonsense, I avoided exploding, and responded; 'Well, put a sign up, then.'

'We shouldn't have to.'

'You have no WiFi,' I began, evenly, 'you have extreme computer use restriction. Be quiet, I'm talking. You'll have your turn when I'm done. You've used up more actual monetary value in the time it took you to even process that thought than it takes to recharge that device, never mind verbalize it. That's how little it costs.'

She began to respond again, somewhat taken aback at lucidity from a hairy, smelly transient. I didn't let her.

'Would you like me to prove it to you? Okay, let me Google it. Oh wait, that's right, I can't, because there's *no bloody WiFi!* Luckily, I have my own portable WiFi hotspot set up, which is one of the reasons I have to charge this battery. Now, maybe if you didn't have *four* librarians working in a small, empty, provincial library, your county council would be able to afford a £12 WiFi router. You've got more staff than Gandalf.' (I'd been waiting to use that one for months, but the opportunity had never presented itself.) I softened a little, 'You should never have tugged on this thread, luv.'

'Actually, I'd be quite interested to see how much it costs, but there's no need to take that tone.'

'An iPhone 5 costs about 1/7th of a penny to completely recharge, and I can prove it. Your objection to my tone is noted.'

I went back the next day. Not because I needed to, as my work was done, just to plug some more shit in.

Luckily, my experience of working outside in the arctic conditions of the Canadian winter stood me in good stead for the hurricane blizzard on the top of Ben Nevis. I've been below -50 Celsius many times, so I knew what to expect.

I was layered up enough to be quite comfortable as long as I kept moving. My fleece gloves and decrepit hiking boots were inadequate, but it was so cold the snow was dry and didn't melt through, which is where the trouble would start.

The peak of the 4,409' Ben Nevis is a plateau a few hundred metres across. The trig point marking the actual summit was on the far side, and the path to it was indicated every fifty yards or so by stone cairns, constructed so climbers wouldn't lose their way in snow or low visibility. (Trig points are concrete bollards atop many topological elevations across the UK to provides platforms for surveying instruments, constructed during the Napoleonic Wars to provide the defenders with detailed maps in case of invasion. There were 6,500 constructed, of which around 6,000 still survive.)

A group of seven of the hardier (or foolhardier) souls, all men, I noted, had congregated at the first cairn at the edge of the plateau, as if at a bus stop, debating whether to carry on. With the addition of me, we had the numbers to form a human chain out into the storm to scan for the next one. This we did, found it, and followed each other there. We repeated the process for the next few, and our GPSs told us we were within 200 metres of the trig point when two of our crew, clearly frightened, asked to turn back. There wasn't much resistance.

On the way down I got talking to a trio of our summiting group who'd been on a three peak odyssey. Over the space of three days, they'd climbed Mount Snowdon, Scafell Pike, and now Ben Nevis (the highest mountains in Wales, England and Scotland respectively), which is seriously impressive going, especially in late October, but not my idea of a vacation at all.

Descending was actually harder than going up, as I was already knackered. My rugby knees started complaining, closely followed by my roofing hip, well before halfway, and my new friends left me far behind.

I hobbled the rest of the way down leaning heavily on my one hiking pole, to arrive at the pub at the bottom like Peachy Carnehan returning from Kafiristan, six hours, ten miles and a thousand years after setting off, just in time to watch England versus Australia in the rugby. Unfortunately, there's no TV at the *Ben Nevis Inn*, and I neglected to ask about WiFi, instead unlocking my bike and gingerly pedalling to *The Crofter* in Fort William, trying to avoid exacerbating my raw bits, my longing for a pint temporarily suspended. It seemed I unconsciously knew if I settled into one at the *Ben* the rugby could've gone and fucked itself.

I got there in time for the second half (England lost despite a spirited performance), then stopped by Morrisons for curry ingredients. The previous week's rain had resulted in the estuary flooding at high tide, but my astute site selection meant my camp was dry, even if getting to it meant riding through a foot of water on the two footbridges. Rule #1: always live on a hill.

It started raining on the way home, and I suddenly remembered today was Halloween. And it was nice to see, in the perpetual transatlantic cultural exchange, the arrival on our green and pleasant shores of the scantily-clad Halloween slut.

And I met a French hiker on the path, who was obviously looking for a campsite in the flooded landscape. I invited him to share my pitch, but he seemed nervous about talking to a large stranger in the dark and in the middle of nowhere. While I was cooking in my tent foyer I heard him wander back and forth in the dark a few more times. I've been there and it sucks. Poor bastard.

So was that first pint worth all this effort?

Absolutely. It always is.

The Caledonian

I get complimented occasionally on how adventurous I'm being, cycling around the world, even though I haven't roamed far yet.

Thing is, I don't consider it particularly adventurous. After all, I'm not visiting anywhere that hasn't been visited before, and I'm going to places people *live*. It's not like I'm hiking across Antarctica, or scaling some great mountain, or I dunno, hanging my toothbrush too close to the toilet. It's possibly the least dangerous thing I've ever done, professionally or otherwise, yet those close to me suddenly express concern. Weird. Were they not paying attention to the last twenty-five years of construction, rugby, mixed martial arts and a thirsty predilection for alcohol-fuelled excess or am I grossly misjudging how dangerous riding a bike along quiet country lanes is? And how hazardous can it be if folks are *living* there?

Maybe it's because I read a lot. When people mention the word 'adventure' to me, I think Conan the Barbarian, not Conan O'Brien, and I often compare what I'm doing to commuting by bike and camping, two activities hardly considered perilous.

It's been suggested to me more than once, however, and usually by coppers, that thieves and muggers may identify me as a target. I think those who consider such things are completely unfamiliar with three particulars of travelling this way:

1. Probably 95% of my time is spent in the countryside and wilderness, where roaming gangs of criminals aren't.

2. The overwhelming majority of people are nice. Police officers and the military are particularly bad at recognizing this, probably because most

of their working days are spent dealing with liars and delinquents, which of course includes members of their own hierarchies as well as the politicians who tell them what to do (I realize it's unfashionable to criticize the military nowadays, if not the police, but I count too many members among my friends not to question their bleak perspective). By contrast, I run the gamut of regular folk daily, from the basest scum to the airiest twat, and am happy to report truly evil people seem rare indeed.

3. Me, personally. I'm quite prepared to fuck a mugger up, and have extensive training and experience in the art of doing so. However, I'm completely aware that multiple assailants form the core of our mugging fraternity's methodology, which is why I bristle with improvised weaponry. My retracted hiking pole is a handy club with telescopic sleeve locking levers that protrude at brutal flesh-ripping angles, and my bike lock a thick chain with a weighty padlock that can serve as a rather intimidating medieval flail. I've not had a single instance of trouble, though I have probably been sized up by potential muggers who decided better of it. In fact, I know I have. One does not acquire nor maintain such immutable swagger without learning a thing or two about such human behaviour.

In addition, the time I spend in towns is fleeting, during daylight, and mostly to buy food. I like that supermarkets are usually on the outskirts, so I can circumvent the innards if I have to, but this is to avoid tiresome navigational issues (such as counterintuitive one-way systems, unmapped brick walls, and in one dramatically profane encounter, a cliff), rather than whatever the admirer might deem dangerous. Most of the time, however, a town will contain at least a couple of things I want to see, and of course a library to work in (which is also kryptonite to the criminal mindset).

Anyway, it was time to leave Fort William.

After a week I'd grown quite fond of the place. The first night I'd met Bricks, and became somewhat melancholy afterwards. Well, not melancholy precisely, contemplative, perhaps? It proved to be a milestone, a waypoint to review my progress towards enlightenment, and I decided I wasn't drinking nearly enough.

I dragged my feet breaking camp, hesitant to leave the convenience of nearby shops, and finally got out of there after two hours and a final lingering look back at the towering Ben Nevis.

It may not be the highest of mountains, internationally speaking, but has a topological prominence to rival many far taller. With a sigh I mounted up and the Caledonian Canal bike path conveyed me directly to *Neptune's Staircase*, a series of locks and swing bridges that form the freshwater entrance to the sixty mile waterway. The canal, two centuries ago, took Thomas Telford and three thousand men nineteen years to build.

Unfortunately the endeavour was never really rewarded with commercial success. By the time it was finished the Napoleonic naval threat was over, the invention of the railway loomed, and the move from wooden hulls to steel saw cargo ships outsize the safe new corridor. Nowadays it is owned by Scottish Waterways and run primarily as a tourist attraction, and a spectacular one it is, too.

A few miles up its length I rode off on a tangent to see the Commando Memorial at Spean Bridge, as recommended by my younger brother Dave, the ex-Royal Marine. This statue has to be situated in one of the most breathtaking spots in the highlands, with a 360 degree view that made me want to shoo off the teary-eyed old codgers moping about the place, flatten the memorial and throw up a log cabin. The only thing stopping me was the threat of swift justice at the hands of the aforementioned, who likely knew a few tricks about terminally dispatching irreverent young men. That and universal ostracisation, of course. Oh, and laws.

On the road back to the canal, I did make mental note of what looked like a small abandoned chapel, too overgrown to really tell, which would certainly work as a fixer-upper. If I ever do settle in one place, this was as fine a location as any.

The Caledonian Canal slices through the middle of Northern Scotland, joining together several linear lochs to create a continuous waterway between the east and west coasts. This tear through the highlands is known as the Great Glen Fault, where two tectonic plates frottage like teenagers on supermarket cider, or at least used to, and still do occasionally, but less enthusiastically. The first of those lochs heading east is Loch Lochy, surely named by either a toddler, managerial groupthink, or some kind of raffle. Further evidence arrived in the name of the next one up, Loch Oich. People were obviously taking the piss, so I rechecked my map. Nope, that's their names.

On the trail I had a quick chat with a hiker labouring under a huge rucksack and heading in the same direction. We met again up the trail at a lochshore campsite, set amid the kind of magnificent mountain scenery that multiples house prices exponentially.

The deserted site had an open-face log bothy for campers, and a ready-built fire to warm us, all gratis. What a remarkably more sensible approach the Scottish Forestry Commission has to campers than its English counterpart, who seems to treat public access to nature with the same distaste most of us reserve for kiddie snuff porn. The contrast is really quite astounding. Scotland throws open its arms and welcomes you in like an old mate, while England slams the door and petulantly charges you to knock. I know where I'd rather be. I felt quite embarrassed to be English at this juncture, particularly because I was in the company of a foreign visitor. Scottish landowners, by simply acting like normal people in pursuit of the greater good, make the English ruling class look like the fucking Ferengi.

Which they are, let's face it.

On returning to England I've broached this subject many times, and several people have curiously tried to defend the official Gollum position of their 'higher ups', citing ludicrous notions like Scotland having fewer people, so it can afford greater hospitality. I've never heard such illogical and loathsome nonsense. It's justifying selfishness and legislating against freedom, nothing more than exasperatingly excusing utterly cunty behaviour.

Anyway.

The hiker's name was Liad, an Israeli climber in his mid-twenties exploring the highlands. He'd hiked and hitched across most of Europe after the end of his military service as a computer dude in the IDF. We decided not to use the bothy as we both preferred the water- and wind-proofing offered by our tents. We camped on the beach and chatted into the night, and he shared some Turkish coffee with me the next morning. He packed up more quickly than I did and set off, while I took a little longer to enjoy the misty alpine scenery.

On the bike I powered up the first hills like a man possessed, despite being unable to access my lowest nine gears (my front derailleur had been playing up the last few days, and I didn't have a clue how to readjust it). I initially put this down to the caffeine jolt from the coffee, but it was more than that. I was sprinting up the slopes like a penis helmet pro, experiencing little in the way of fatigue. I was finally getting fit, that's what it was! It'd been so long I'd forgotten the feeling. Like a cardio maniac I relished the uphills even more than usual, attacking them all the more aggressively, pushing myself to see where my new limits were. I couldn't reach them. Overnight, somehow I'd gone from a struggling wimp to a thunderous explosion of muscle, barely contained by sinew, bone and skin. I was svelte, powerful, and the master of all I pedalled. My lungs laughed at hardship. My heart pumped anew. My thighs roared at the mountains like great swooping beasts. I'd never felt such physical elation!

As I neared the village of Laggan I dismounted for a farm gate, and, epic plonkerdom ever ready to pounce, realized I'd left my loaded trailer back at the campsite.

I sheepishly retrieved the thing and found the return journey distinctly less worthy of comment. I pushed on towards Fort Augustus, passing the curious and temporarily closed *Eagle Barge Inn*, a pub on a barge. I'd planned to work here, but wasn't too miffed as rain threatened and I wanted to make more progress before camping.

Several miles on the trail on the east side of Loch Oich became too roughly strewn with tree roots to ride over. My rig could probably handle it, but water bottles kept bouncing from beneath their bungees and I lost another one I didn't hear hit the ground. I got off and pushed. Navigating a gated bridge (where I have to prop up the bike, open the gate, push through, reprop, close, unprop and carry on) the hiking pole I use as a kickstand slipped on the mossy footing and the rig keeled over, snapping the footlong pivot pin that attaches the trailer arms to the body of the trailer.

I did some swearing and then silently despaired for several minutes, considering whom I should call to come and rescue me, but shut that shit down with a finality that frankly surprised me. I was ten miles from nowhere. Construction Foreman Stef took over. I unloaded the trailer, surveyed the damage, and began to formulate repairs with the resources I had available.

Just then, who should come down the path but Liad and a freshly befriended female backpacker, a Canadian girl called Emily. They had missed the next turning and had to backtrack, discovering my predicament. Liad stopped to help out while Emily kept going, citing a pressing rendezvous, and we managed to jerry rig a replacement pin from two tent pegs, wedged in place by a length of paracord, wound with duct tape and bound by a tight bungee. Not perfect, but I figured it would get me to a metal fabrication shop in Inverness, not that I had enough money for such extravagances, you understand. I needed to get online and canvass for some more writing work.

Liad headed off as I repacked. I took the wrong turn and had to double back myself, catching him about an hour later. The boy moved fast for carrying such a huge pack. Back on the trail we decided on a canalside patch of grass for a campsite. Darkness was descending on nearby Fort Augustus, so we headed into the village for the small supermarket without pitching our tents first, which turned out to be a mistake as it began to rain on the way back. In changeable weather when deciding on a tent pitch, it's always best to get one's shelter up at the first fair opportunity. I don't get wet while camping or even on the bike so much, it's during the transitions. So we got soaked. Liad got his tent up first, and then helped with mine as the rain bucketed down. I'm not sure I would've done the same, and felt both humbled and inspired by his fellowship.

I set up the candle heaters to desperately try to dry out gloves, socks and boots, and had a £1.49 tin of Morrisons Irish Stew for dinner, which I wasn't looking forward to as tinned meals tend to smell a bit like dog food when you open them up. The stew, however, was a thoroughly pleasant surprise. Very tasty, and mopped up with some fresh bread I couldn't have been happier. I think I've found my brand. I finished off my repast with a box of Mr. Kipling's Chocolate Slices and a few chocolate digestives, washed down with a cup of coffee, and snuggled up in my sleeping bag to listen to the rain. The sky was clear the next morning, and Fort Augustus is gorgeous. The sunrise dramatically lit the mountains, streaking shadows across their faces at such acute angles they actually seemed to frown and smile.

Liad again finished packing first and headed to the coffee shop, while I took my time to enjoy the surroundings and idly chatted with passing locals. I caught up with him at the village bridge and we said our goodbyes, as he headed for the Isle of Skye and I continued on the Caledonian, promising to visit him in Israel.

In glorious sunshine, the cycle route followed the road here onto the east side of Loch Ness, up into the highlands and away from the incredibly blue water, a dash of cobalt rapture in the roiling mountains. It was some serious climbing, and most of the morning and early afternoon were spent off the bike and pushing (I still hadn't adjusted my front derailleur, primarily because I didn't want to fuck it up further. I needed to get to somewhere with WiFi so I could watch a YouTube instructional or two). The rain started up mid-morning and set in for the day, sousing the dramatic views with, I like to think, a hint of sorrow.

After two hours of punishing gradients the miles of downhills began, and swept me into the pub in the village of Whitebridge. I got there at 2.35pm, however, and they closed at 3pm, but the barman invited me to stay in the hotel lounge to dry off, such was my sopping condition. What considerate people. I got the fire going and began the process of drying out, meanwhile breaking out my laptop to put some proposals in on prospective writing jobs, and watch the first of a few videos to decipher the mysteries of bike gearing.

After three hours or so most of my kit was dry and the rain had stopped. So I packed up and rejoined the downhills, and found a very fetching spot to camp among the ferns by a tumbling burn outside the mountainside village of Foyer. I fell asleep excited by the prospect of the next day's descent and ride along the shores of Loch Ness.

War and patriotism

'You're hauling too much stuff.'

'Nah,' I contradicted the experienced cycle tourist I'd been talking to for the last thirty minutes. We were chatting at one of the trailer-blocking bridleway entrance obstacles of which overeager planning departments are so frustratingly fond, 'I'm hauling too much stuff *for you.*'

I suspended cathartic visions of a brutal council office axe massacre and softened the insult with a grin. 'If I'm not complaining, it shouldn't bother you, either. I like my kitchen sink.'

'But wouldn't you prefer to ride further every day?'

'I'm not particularly about seeing as much stuff as quickly as possible, mate, I'm not on a vacation. It's about the journey, experiences, and living in the moment,' I said with more conviction than I felt. But then decided I was right.

When I get in my tent, it's my home from home, rather than a temporary respite from the elements, which is why I use a large two person rather than a single, and I'm actually thinking of moving up to a three person, because that's how I roll, bitches. Pimping in a guest wing, if you will. Most tent manufacturers are laughably conservative about sleeping capacities, so cycle tourists typically use a size up. Solo riders will use a two person, couples a three, etc, but I require more space. In addition, load-wise I carry up to ten litres of water and a week of food, so I can stop anywhere I fancy on a whim, and two stoves so I can make more elaborate meals. I have many redundancies built in, and lots of stuff I've never used, such as certain tools that take up space but would be invaluable during a mechanical crisis in the middle of nowhere.

Do I curse the weight on a steep hill? Not really, no more than I do any other exercise; I'm in no hurry. This is something a lot of proper cycle tourists, irrevocably bungeed to day jobs and minacious mortgages, and voracious families, fail to grasp: Being an aimless vagabond is my *work*, now, such as it is. I'm the job, my brain's the game, and soaking up juicy information and substantive experiences the goal. And besides, enduring a little cardio slogging up a hill is redemption for the indulgence. It eases the grudging guilt of euphoric downhills, rapturous scenery, unctuous cakes, endless candy, witnessing history, geography and culture unfold from a tangible first person perspective far superior to any academic deliberation, and every one I climb makes me fitter, and the next one more surmountable. It's a win-win-win. Without uphill struggles I'd be all soft yin and empty yang. Without the suck, the joy would seem less so. One must embrace the suck, even revel in it. And the suck ends at the summit.

The challenging highlands of Scotland are a comparatively deserted region. At just over nine people per square kilometre it's one of the most sparsely populated areas in Europe. At least, this is what Wikipedia claims. 'But what about northern Scandinavia?' I roared indignantly at this often derided source, 'or Eastern Europe?' I looked it up elsewhere, and by Jiminy, they were right.

The numbers were much higher in previous centuries, but upheavals such as the Highland Clearances (where powerful landowners forcibly enclosed common land for their own use, effectively marooning smaller subsistence farmers, possibly one of the most criminal moves by the upper class in Britain's turbulent history) and the industrial revolution saw huge swathes move to the coasts and lowlands, as well as significant numbers abroad to North America and Australasia. Interestingly, there are more descendants of Highlanders in these locations than remain in Scotland, a notion I was noticing in overheard accents. Occasionally I'd mistake Scots for American if I snatched just a snippet, tuned as I am to the US vernacular. This suggests to me there's a disproportionate descendance of Scottish in the American linguistic stew, which I'd certainly look up on Google if I was interested enough to be arsed.

Another late start due to the increasingly frequent rain. At noon I left my scenic roost above the torrential river Foyers, itself created by a confluence of the wonderfully named rivers Gourag and Fechlin, and descended from the heights along one of General Wade's famed military roads, through the mountainside village of Foyers itself, down to the pretty shores of Loch Ness.

These roads were laid in the 18th century to aid troop movement during the highland Jacobite Risings. It's difficult to imagine such violent contention in such a beatific setting, but demonstrates how silly people can be when the ridiculous carrot-and-stickfest of money and power are involved. The Duke of Hanover, William of Orange, had a claim on the British throne and made one at the head of 15,000 men. There was little opposition from the nobles in England, primarily because the Duke agreed to uphold the ratifications of the *Magna Carta* and the establishment of the *Bill of Rights*, which ultimately reduced the power of the monarchy to a constitutional figurehead. The deposed Catholic James II preferred absolute power, believing it divinely granted, a ludicrous notion inherited by the equally unenlightened Bonnie Prince Charlie. The Prince personifying the invention of 'country' and became a rallying cry for Scottish patriotism. Patriotism is an ideology I've long curated but never quite embraced.

George Bernard Shaw suggested '*Patriotism is your conviction that this country is superior to all other countries because you were born in it*', neatly summating my feelings on the subject. If you're a patriot, do you honestly believe the group of people you artificially affiliate with, formally designated by lines drawn on maps by politicians, are somehow *special*? There's two words for that, my provincial friend, and those words are 'simple' and 'ego'.

Look, we're cave people, and have been for millions of years. Now we just build our own. Unless we're attached by blood or friendship, you ain't in my tribe. We lived in small nomadic hunter-gatherer bands of twenty or thirty members for millions of years; a hundred thousand generations (compared to around four hundred since the advent of agriculture). These small groups would associate with similarly-sized groups whose ranges overlapped. *That's* our tribe: our family and neighbouring friends. Anthropologists have discovered the number of people we can develop meaningful relationships with to be about 150 or so, known as *Dunbar's Number*, which remains fairly constant despite our surroundings: those living rurally cast their net further afield, while those in urban settings rarely speak to the folks next door. Countries, by comparison, are barely a few generations old and millions strong. That ain't our tribe at all. Not even close.

I can't help but feel General George Wade should be a more interesting bloke. He was born in Ireland, and such was his solid if not spectacular military and political career, that he received a mention in the lyrics of the national anthem around 1745. He was sufficiently mediocre to became a very popular MP, representing the well-heeled people of Bath from 1722 until his death in 1748. To be honest, the most interesting thing about him is he died unmarried but with three kids. So he was very probably a rake, which for me is a tick in the plus column.

Lord, grant that Marshal Wade
May, by thy mighty aid,
Victory bring.
May he sedition hush
And, like a torrent, rush
Rebellious Scots to crush.
God save the King.

This tribute obviously didn't go down too well north of the border, and the verse was scrapped. Wade's opposition to Bonnie Prince Charlie (whose belief in this 'divine right of kings' rubbish puts him firmly in the cunt camp, making his deified folk hero status all the more exasperating) supported the swelling movement towards democracy in Great Britain, and culminated at the 1746 Battle of Culloden, the last pitched battle fought on British soil.

Had you seen these roads before they were made,
You would lift up your hands and bless General Wade

I dawdled along the waterside for most of the afternoon, contemplating this history and the second largest loch in Scotland by area (22 square miles), and largest by volume (755 feet deep, Loch Ness contains more fresh water than all the lakes of England and Wales combined) before leaving its northern banks behind for the highland capital of Inverness.

Another shower shepherded me into a bus shelter on the outskirts, and I spent the time Google Streetviewing potential wild campsites. I found one just around the corner, close to a Tesco, and decided to do a quick food shop while the rain passed.

Sometimes, in my daily visits to the supermarket, I experience a kind of reality warp. I enter with a clearly delineated shopping list of, for example, bogroll, matches, tinned soup and a loaf of bread, and emerge with a packet of Bourbon creams, an apple turnover, three onions and a banana.

This transmogrification occurs, I'm sure, because of special offers. When on a limited budget, special offers spring tumescently to the fore like misplaced porn in the Disney aisle. Several British supermarkets have got into the commendable habit of grouping their specials together in one place, especially perishables nearing their sell-by date. I plunder such bays like a Viking berserker, pausing to ask myself 'do I like cheese coleslaw?' and 'what exactly is hummus?' amid the raging red mist.

Settled and fed in the tent I decided to engage Shawn, a good Texan lawyer friend of mine, on Facebook in a perfunctory squabble about something. I picked the provocative topic of vegetables in chilli con carne, as he prides himself on his own authentic southwestern US recipe that scorns the tomato but desperately clings to the abuses of onion. We share similar views on pretty much everything, so we regularly invent stuff to argue about. I suggested starting off with a *mirepoix*, a chopped mixture of onion, celery and carrot used as a base in French soups, sauces and stews, to round out the flavour profile. He disagreed and said some scandalous things about British cuisine. I won, of course. He disagreed with that, too.

I put my bag down by reception to sign up, only to discover the Inverness library had no WiFi. I wordlessly gaped at the librarian for a couple of seconds, fourteen years into the 21st century and all, then asked if they had a study area where I could plug in.

'Well, the problem is, you see,' she said, 'our wiring is so old we're asking people not to plug anything in, as the fuses might blow and it's a safety concern.'

Utter fucking dogshit. Another council simulating fiscal responsibility for the dumber voter by alienating people who are suddenly surprisingly prepared to burn the place down tonight. 'You're saying my laptop will blow this entire building's electrical infrastructure?'

'Yes.'

'I've been cycling around Scotland for six weeks, navigating electronically, and this is the first library I've encountered with no WiFi and a plug ban. Are you seriously suggesting a phone charger will blow the lot?'

'Yes.' But there was a crack there, quickly camouflaged by obstinance. My coherence obviously didn't jive with my roguish appearance.

'Well, if I get lost and die in a highland blizzard because I haven't charged my GPS,' I huffed, turning to dramatically depart on the last word, 'I'm coming back to haunt your children.' Pleased with this devastating rejoinder, I promptly tripped over my backpack.

I put her reticence down to my lack of cycling gear (I was discovering people treated me less like a transient when I was wearing my cock helmet or luminous twat jersey: note to self), and Google mapped a route to the next nearest library in Culloden. I managed twenty minutes of charging there before they closed for a bafflingly mediterraneanesque two hour lunch.

I decided to visit the nearby Culloden battlefield on Drumossie Moor instead of waiting for them to reopen, but the long climb out of the village dissuaded my return. I bimbled around the battlefield for a bit, learning as much as I could about a conflict of which I was fairly ignorant. Turns out the discipline of the English broke the fury of the French-and-Irish-supported Highlanders, largely because of the bayonet drill which involved each redcoat in the line attacking the Highlander to his right, rather than the one straight ahead, thereby bypassing the Scottish shields once their charge hit. At least, that's the story. I toyed with the idea of camping here, but there were too many people about, so I set off south into the Cairngorms.

Just before starting the first major ascent, I stumbled upon the *Clava Cairns*, a series of stone burial mounds dating back to 2,000BC. What a find! This is precisely why I've fallen in love with travelling this way. I nosed around the deserted site for an hour, taking photographs and imagining the neolithic builders hard at work. I considered disobeying the 'No Camping' sign, as this place was suitably remote and pitching away from the road would be hidden by darkness, but decided to push on up into the mountains as I still had juice in the legs, and there was some daylight left.

An hour of climbing finished me off, and I made a particularly cosy camp in a pine forest, resting on years of softly layered pine needles.

The only power I had left was 20% on my phone, so I shut it down, lit a candle, and wrote old school, with pen and paper, until the cold numbed my fingers.

Everything was frozen this morning. All my water, the overnight flysheet condensation, and the sweaty clothes I'd hung on the lower tree boughs to dry. I hunted down a stream to grab some water for a wash, and it was Narnian solid. Yikes. I took a Wet Wipes whore's bath instead, but my distrusting testicles snatched up into my torso like a *Kung Fu* pebble grab, spectacularly flipping me into the air with the recoil. I picked myself up and coaxed them back out with soft cooing, talcum powder, and the snug promise of warm winter cycling tights.

The low sun hit the icy road about 10am, and it began to thaw. I set off with twenty-five miles to go to Aviemore, Scotland's attempt at a ski resort. I'd never been there, but was fascinated to see how crap it might be. I found a data signal atop a rise and discovered the town library closed at four, and as I was desperate to recharge my electronics, I put the hammer down. The bicycle route follows the A9 in a roundabout way, so much so it became frustrating as today wasn't about pleasant riding, but about getting to my destination, the search for enlightenment temporarily suspended. When the route began to double back on itself yet again, I fucked it and took to the shoulderless A95 for the last four or five miles, which delivered me directly into the centre of Aviemore, albeit a little shaken up.

I don't like riding on major roads at the best of times, but my frustration with the bike path eclipsed my common sense. There's nothing like a few close passes from 70 mph HGVs to rapidly revitalize one's faith in gentler thoroughfares. It's not a lack of confidence in my riding ability, you understand, it's the putting my life in the hands of people I've never met who can kill me with a mere lapse in concentration.

The larger part of the Cairngorms National Park consists of several broad plateaus, but actually looks like one large one. This means the cycling is mostly flat, but is fetchingly surrounded by some of the tallest mountains in Britain. Scotland's second highest peak after Ben Nevis, Ben MacDui, is part of the range, 114 feet shorter than its big brother. Local people for years planned to pile stones on the top in a fascinatingly futile attempt to claim the title for the uncaring crag, a stunningly lopsided example of cost-benefit analysis, and obviously a silent and lonely cry for validation. If your hobby involves carrying rocks up a hill, folks, chances are your life is in need of stern redirection.

I decided not to climb it when I discovered Queen Victoria had done so in 1859, and figured if she was capable it couldn't be much of a challenge. She wrote 'It had a sublime and solemn effect, so wild, so solitary—no one but ourselves and our little party there . . . I had a little whisky and water, as the people declared pure water would be too chilling.'

I've since discovered she rode up on a pony, which is, of course, cheating. Ben MacDui is also home to *Am Fear Liath Mòr*, AKA the *Big Grey Man of Ben MacDui*, a bigfoot-like creature that apparently haunts the frequent mists. He was first reported in 1925 by noted mountaineer J. Norman Collie, who was also a PhD in chemistry and Fellow of the Royal Society, so he was far from being a nutjob. He wrote: 'I began to think I heard something else than merely the noise of my own footsteps. For every few steps I took I heard a crunch, and then another crunch as if someone was walking after me but taking steps three or four times the length of my own' ... 'the eerie crunch, crunch, sounded behind me, I was seized with terror and took to my heels, staggering blindly among the boulders for four or five miles.'

Highland whisky, finest in the world.

I had a hard time finding the library, as Google maps placed it right by the road, when it is, in fact, set down a side street and hidden in a school/sports complex. I stubbornly rode through the village three times before relenting and asking a local. I did, however, discover Aviemore to be a very pretty place, European ski resort in appearance, with a plethora of alpine bars, hotels, and restaurants. I was itching to go on the piss, because a pub crawl in this place could become the stuff of legend, but I needed to get myself out of the mountains before the real winter hit, and going out on the blather at my age is a three day event.

Once in the library I plugged everything in and basked in the warmth. There was no WiFi and no data signal, but there were online computers, so I Googled around for a campsite and decided to bed down in some woods by the train tracks, very near the library, so I could be back in here first thing. Charging up all my stuff takes a full day, but I could ratchet up a workable chunk in the 10am-4pm Sunday opening hours tomorrow.

While updating my Facebook, an old neighbour of mine from Scarborough I hadn't seen for thirty years messaged me. She lived in Aviemore with her husband, and wanted to come to the library and say hello. Gail turned up about ten minutes later and we had a lovely chat for an hour or so. She kissed me on the cheek goodbye and I had to admire her bravery; my road funk was an obnoxious wall by now. I really needed to have a proper wash and launder.

I camped down literally ten feet from the train track, which proved intriguing. In the familiar environment of my tent I would forget, and be deep into a movie, when the ground would vibrate, almost imperceptibly, then rapidly explode into an impossibly deafening maelstrom of noise and light. I experienced a psychologically cleansing second of pure bowel-loosening terror each time before remembering where I was. This was going to be interesting in the morning.

It was. There's nothing quite like being woken up by what initially appears to be a planet-killing meteor strike. The intense wave of endorphins that follows such a pronounced adrenalin spike is palpably psychedelic. You can keep your base-jumping and heroin nonsense, camp next to a railway.

It was very cold. So cold, in fact, when I rode to the library the bike slipped on some invisible black ice and the rig went down like a Latin centre forward. My head smacked the pavement with significant prejudice. Luckily I was wearing my cock helmet so no damage was done to the tarmac.

After the library shut I went on a cookie hunt, managing to corner some digestives, ginger nuts, and custard creams in, funnily enough, a corner shop. I absently munched on them back in the tent. Three cups of coffee and an episode of *Star Trek* later, they were all gone, and that was dinner.

A lot of my friends have expressed jealously at what I'm doing, and admittedly, there's a lot to be jealous of, but cookie dinners may well top the list.

Science and The Wolf

So what exactly is the Higgs Boson Particle?

Probably not a question you'd expect from some roving tentamuffin, and certainly not in a Cairngorms travelogue. The reason I bring it up is because it was while walking in these very mountains in 1964, Peter Higgs, a Geordie from Newcastle-upon-Tyne and lecturer at the Tait Institute of Mathematical Physics at the University of Edinburgh, developed his hypothesis of the *Higgs Mechanism*, which defies detailed explanation because I don't understand a bloody word.

In a nutshell, however, I'm told it's the part of the *Standard Model of Particle Physics* (itself a devilish whirligig of words, integers, and peculiar mathematical doodads) that lends matter the property of *mass*. Without the Higgs Mechanism everything in the universe would be flitting about at light speed and stuff wouldn't, well, *be*. Which is why the party at CERN's Large Hadron Collider, when the mechanism was finally confirmed in 2013, must've been a knees-up to shame even my own nefarious drinking buddies. There would have been the poking of flashing red buttons marked DANGER, drunken dares to quaff antimatter projects and cosmos-collapsing cries of the Universal Disaster Portent; *Watch this, lads!*

I like to imagine a frail octogenarian Peter Higgs, surrounded by giggling science groupies and prostrate academics, when, spectacles dislodged by the bounce of an errant boob and draped in party popper ejaculate, he murmurs his now legendary maxim, 'It's very nice to be right sometimes.'

These scenarios obviously wouldn't occur, of course, as the great unwashed (and the great washed, for that matter) are too distracted by the bling of celebrity show business, shouty sporting events and the gloom of war and catastrophe to attend the properly important. Our water cooler conversations concentrate on Bieber's new 'do, or outrage at the latest infantile/anemic government policy, or whether some red carpet trollop inhaled the wrong cock when her career began to flag. Higgs et al didn't register even the tiniest blip on most people's radar.

Higgs' wandering demonstrates the benefit of imagination, and more poignantly, the importance of having the opportunity to explore it. One of the problems, I feel, with modern western life is our lack of this luxury. Every waking moment seems to be filled with some distraction or other. Even while strolling to the corner shop I feel compelled to fill the time with music or an entertaining podcast. While partaking of such things may be intellectually and emotionally appealling, they rarely improve our implicit ability to reason, or help us arrive at a considered opinion. As I've grown and matured (shut up), I've found myself less reluctantly agreeing with the older generation that silence is the best soundtrack for thinking.

The sharp cold dulled somewhat, the deficit replaced by blustery waves of misting rain, necessitating several flappy and frozen-fingered fights with the poncho. I thus stuttered along the undulating bike route to Kingussie while listening to an episode of the *Joe Rogan Podcast* about weird people preempting the inevitable mergence of technology and biology by sewing magnets under their skin, followed by a chapter of Bernard Cornwell's *Harlequin* (AKA *The Archer's Tale* in the US), which put me in a receptive mood for something historical. The Highlands didn't disappoint.

Ruthven Barracks appeared from behind a hill and stopped me in my tracks. This gem of a ruin is sited on a hill dominating the middle of a broad valley and surrounded by mountains: it's got *Game of Thrones* written all over it, in a location not unlike Edoras, the capital of Rohan from the *Lord of the Rings* movies. I hadn't seen a car or person in twenty minutes, so I parked up by the gate, didn't even bother locking up the rig, and clambered up the steep path to find out what the hell this place was. The sign said it was a barracks completed in 1721 by our old mate General Wade to house soldiers combating the Jacobite Uprising.

It was besieged twice, the first time defending against 300 Jacobites with only 12 redcoats, the second time overrun by Bonnie Prince Charlie's minions. After their defeat at the Battle of Culloden in 1746, they had subsequently made this their rally point some forty odd miles away. Three thousand highlanders gathered here after the fight, to be met by a message to disperse from the aspiring potentate. I was starting to dislike this posh pretend Scottish git more and more. He didn't even have the stones to show up himself. They set fire to the place when they left, and what stands now is pretty much what remained.

There's something incredibly satisfying about exploring a deserted ruin alone. It lends a unique solitude and reflection, absent with company, that stirs the imagination and helps transport oneself back in time. It's difficult to comprehend, just 250 years ago, this was a military outpost, in hostile territory, on *our own island.* Now, 250 years might seem like a long time to the rest of the English-speaking world, but in this neck of the global woods, it's as good as last week.

While exploring the two barracks blocks, devoid now of furniture, floors and roof, I still got a sense of what life must've been like for the soldiers, crowded in ten to a room and two to a bed. The stables to the rear of the fort catered to the dragoon rapid reaction force, tasked to keep the roads clear of bothersome autocrats.

The barracks are built on the bones of an earlier castle, one of the lairs of Alexander Stewart, the Earl of Buchan. This hate-filled fuckwit was known as the *Wolf of Badenoch* in the late fourteenth century, primarily because he, along with his *Cateran*, or private army, had a propensity for the rape, pillage and murder of his peasant protectorate that far exceeded the potential ravages of any likely invader. With over forty illegitimate offspring it's difficult to picture the impotent, innocuous nobility of today descending from such lusty and loathsome stock, but this is where inbreeding gets us, I suppose.

As the third son of King Robert II of Scotland, his appalling behaviour was largely tolerated, although token penance was undertaken occasionally to assuage the demands of the Church. He was granted governmental positions and titles such as *Justiciar of Scotia* for a time, likely in an attempt to give the wayward lad some responsibility, but none of it worked. The Wolf's depredations culminated in the sacking and burning of Elgin town and Cathedral in 1390, apparently in retaliation for the Church's condemnation of his murdering, thieving, torturing, and relentless shagging, but more probably the denouement of their power struggle for control of Scotland's north.

One particular story involved imprisoning the monk who delivered the news of Alexander's excommunication in the bottle dungeon of Lochindorb castle. The dungeon breached the water table of the lake island location, meaning any prisoner had to live in three feet of water, essentially sentencing them to a horrible death either by, or caused by, sleep deprivation.

The Wolf was killed, it is said, after losing a game of chess to the Devil himself in 1405 (or 1406, or 1394, depending on who you listen to) at the age of 62 (or 63, or 51), his body found after a great storm marking the Devil's victory, uninjured but with the nails ripped out of his boots. This is, of course, absolute bullshit, but he's interred, rather ironically given his history of psychopathic excess, down the road at Dunkeld Cathedral.

I parked outside the library in Kingussie (population: 1,400), setting for the *Monarch of the Glen* TV series, and noticed another loaded touring bike locked to a railing. I got talking to the chap inside, easily identifiable by his rangy and unkempt contentment. He was a young man for a bicycle tourist, barely into his twenties, and he'd impressively ridden all the way from Istanbul. I loaned him my spare pump to fix a flat, and told him to keep it to see him home to Edinburgh. I gave him my card so he could mail it back to me later.

Ego buffed to an immaculate sheen by such prodigious charity, I left the library as the sun waned and rode to Newtonmore (population: 1,000), the next town along, for a quick shop of bread and cookies, then headed out the other side to camp. Pickings were slim, however, and as darkness fell my anxiety grew until I found a spot by a bend in the B9150. My description of the town should end here, as I'd sluttishly treated the place like a pitstop, but it really is more important than that: Newtonmore being a hotbed of the ancient and amateur sport of shinty.

I first rode past an impressive shinty stadium in Fort William, and was surprised to discover there's an entire sporting league on the island I grew up on that I'd never heard of, despite it predating Christianity. The game has striking similarities to Irish hurling, so much so the sports are often combined under unified rules to allow teams from both to play each other.

Shinty resembles field hockey in a lot of ways, except the ball may be played in the air, and both sides of the stick are used. What's interesting is this little known sport was once far more popular, and was played throughout Britain and her colonies; indeed, Scottish soldiers stationed in Canada would play on the uninterrupted space of frozen lakes, giving rise to the sport of ice hockey.

Newtonmore Camanachd is one of the premier club teams in shinty, and ruled the roost for many decades, winning 30 national championships since the competition's inception in 1896; however, the team from Kingussie, literally two miles away, has dominated the last twenty years or so, winning 23 times in all and meriting a mention in the *2005 Guinness Book of World Records* as the *World sport's most successful sporting team of all time.* What a fascinating yearly rivalry this must be, in this remote and seemingly sedate highland valley. I may have to come back just to go on the piss, I mean, watch a game.

The rain didn't let off until noon again, then I decamped and began a long, cold, granny gear slog into an abject cunt of a headwind, accompanied by stinging horizontal sleet, past the village of Dalwhinnie and its namesake whisky distillery, the highest in Scotland, and up towards the Pass of Drumochter.

I don't complain about much, which is probably an undesirable trait in a writer. Reading a good bitch about something mundane can be hugely entertaining, a revel in someone else's angst whether we empathize with it or not, but there's nothing mundane about a proper headwind for a cyclist. Every revolution becomes a battle, every mile a war. I'd have camped down and waited it out, because I'm all about having fun and this certainly wasn't, but real winter was clawing at my tail and with limited supplies I didn't want to get trapped in the mountains by the snow.

Midway through the pass, frozen and exhausted, the cycle path ended, so I was forced, rather worryingly, onto the A9's dual carriageway. I wasn't crapping myself at every passing lorry for long, however, as roadwork bollards soon separated the lanes. The inside one had been resurfaced, richly dark, lounge singer smooth, and gloriously all to myself for the next ten miles or so of resplendent downhill. In addition, the sleet stopped, the wind switched direction, and the sun smashed through. Thus the breathtaking glide down the broad Garry and Tummel river valleys as they twisted through the mountains was sublime, effortlessly sweeping from pleasing view to pleasing view, a high banked flight corralled by the black ribbon of road. It was hypnotic. Familiar now, I surrendered to it, bathing in the feeling. Not thinking, I turned off the music that'd helped me up the pass and just... flowed. Suddenly, the answer to the question of my life was glaringly obvious. Just do this. Bugger all that other shit. This is what it's about, evermore sweetened by the antecedent slog.

As the land flattened and the bullshit babble of humanity rushed back in, I considered the euphoria. It was an excruciatingly addictive drug. So this is what religion must feel like, I mused. Or heroin. It ruined any further chance of a normal life, whatever that is. I was actually, truly, finally, free.

I considered the aesthetic, too. Was it the simplicity of moving through a gorgeous landscape that caused this, or was this just the first time I'd properly been 'in the moment' on a downhill? And what is 'beauty', anyhow? Realizing I was teetering on the edge of philosophy I knew precious little about, and no doubt every idea I could come up with had already been discussed and dissected to death, I consulted the Greeks and their academic progeny. And discovered the philosophy of aesthetics to be an unnecessarily complicated load of old bollocks, compounding the idea that much of academia invests in overblown waffle to describe things that are quite simple, probably in an attempt to appear brainier. I promptly gave up and decided to sling a quote your way instead to look like I know what I'm talking about.

Beauty is anything you are compelled to look at. - *John Waters*

That should cover it.

I rejoined the bike path, and quickly found a fantastic camping spot on a cliff with a grandstand view of the raging River Garry, a few miles northwest of the awesomely appellated village of Killiecrankie. This has nothing to do with Wee Jimmie Krankie, the cross-dressed Scottish schoolboy of *Crackerjack* fame, but it made me think of her anyway. (She recently admitted, along with her comedy partner and husband Ian, to being heavily involved in the swinging scene during the eighties. Oh, how I curse my persistent and overly vivid imagination.) I clambered down the rock face to grab a bucket of water from a tributary burn, feeling very Bear Grylls, filtered some to drink and had a rejuvenating wash with the rest. Bubbly TV chef Ainsley Harriott completed today's weird celebrity quotient by providing dinner in a packet of his Thai chicken soup, and surprisingly acceptable it was too, hungrily scoffed down with half a loaf of bread. My phone told me it was 4 degrees C in nearby Pitlochry, but the ice in my water bottle disagreed, so I wrapped up cozily and delved deeply into season four of *The Wire*, punctuated by long stares at a fantastic night sky.

Rain forced only a couple of hours in the saddle the next day, but that short span took in a parade of pretty villages, impressive castles and hidden stately homes, the latter often only indicated by their roadside gatehouses, which were pretty spectacular in themselves.

I decided not to stop at Pitlochry library and pushed on through Dunkeld, passing by the cathedral grave of the Wolf of Badenoch, to the library at Birnam, a small village in a fetching valley setting. The library was a throwback to the seventies, it seemed, with an ancient computer system and barely an hour's grace with their ridiculously inconvenient opening schedule. I left with the dark and climbed the valley side along a bike route that looked worrying like a private driveway, confirmed about halfway up by a PRIVATE ROAD sign. Bike routes often follow such prohibited thoroughfares, though, as the signs often only refer to powered transport, so I paid it no mind. I couldn't find a decent flat bit suitable for a tent apart from one right by the road on a corner, but it was so quiet I decided to pitch anyway, and didn't see a soul until morning.

Stefan Abrutat and the Stone of Destiny

I must've gone wrong somewhere.

It's a symptom of my stubbornness, I suppose, to be paracording my bicycle rig piecemeal down a sheer cliff, feeling very Indiana Jones but looking much more Mugshot Nick Nolte, rather than backtracking to find the bike path I had, my petulant GPS insisted, lost.

Many people would put my recalcitrance down to laziness, I imagine, and I'd have to agree, because I'd had a tiring push up the leeward slope and didn't relish undoing all that work. But I prefer to think of my current predicament in terms of Rocky Balboa's motivational speech in his final movie (though there's rumblings, at the time of writing, of yet another one):

> Let me tell you something you already know. The world ain't all sunshine and rainbows. It's a very mean and nasty place and I don't care how tough you are, it will beat you to your knees and keep you there permanently if you let it. You, me, or nobody is gonna hit as hard as life. But it ain't about how hard you hit. It's about how hard you can get hit and keep moving forward. How much you can take and keep moving forward! That's how winning is done!

This creates the illusion I'm personifying the kind of moxie one sees in heroic fiction. Were Rocky actually here, of course, I'm sure he'd punch me right in the mouth for using his sensationalism as an excuse for this stupid shortcut, but he isn't, so fuck that slack-jawed cocksucker.

I clambered down after my stuff, reassembled everything, and began hacking through undergrowth, braying at fallen trees, and deciding medieval merchant-adventuring must've been an act of desperation born of an absolute inability to do anything else. As Marco Polo et al plummeted in my estimation I eventually found the elusive bike path and a sign saying Perth was twelve miles away, whereas the adjacent but shoulderless A9 roadsign said eight. It was early and traffic was light, so I took the less meandering but infinitely more dangerous option, lucking out when the sidewalk began about halfway along, snatching me from the sphincter-puckering terror of near misses.

Sure, cycling on a footway is illegal in the UK and the US, but no way am I needlessly risking my neck for some absent twat of a lawmaker. Moreover, British coppers, rightly and overwhelmingly, ignore this particular infraction, requiring either excruciating personal pedantry or some querulous political quota to issue a ticket. I wouldn't begrudge receiving one, to be honest, and might even welcome the inconvenience just for the opportunity to vociferously assault such pettiness in a courtroom full of people too dim to find a proper job.

Which is rich, coming from me.

Perth is the home of Scone Abbey, which has sadly nothing to do with a surfeit of delicious pastries served with jam and clotted cream, and everything to do with the *Stone of Destiny*, which is very LARPy indeed. I've recently been amusing myself with the notion that the majority of human society actually moves through the real world in exactly the same way as LARPers, playing roles only relevant contextually while wearing similarly outlandish costumes (uniforms, for example. We tend to see these as quite acceptable until we travel abroad, ridicule the exotic pomposity of the Banana Republic uniforms there, then suddenly realize our own are equally daft), somewhat akin to the Shakespearean idea that all the world's a stage. This doesn't make their conventional version of reality* any more valid, of course. The only real difference is mundanes (gamers' epithet for non-gamers) actually hurt, inconvenience, imprison, and kill people. You can probably begin to see why the more facets of establishment I experience while travelling, the more objective my perspective becomes, and the more my respect for authority continues to spiral towards smacking some clipboard ponce for standing in my way.

*Reality is very weird shit. Consider, for a moment, your brain. It interprets the universe through your senses, but doesn't tell you what you are really experiencing, which is a huge collection of molecules in various states of agitation, the volume of which, in any state outside the density of stuff like black holes, white dwarfs, and neutron stars, is mostly empty space. For example, if a hydrogen nucleus (a single proton) was the size of a marble, its lone electron would be an orbiting spec of dust half a mile away, making the entire atom 99.9999999999996% nothingness. Thus, for example, when we touch something, we actually don't. The atoms in our fingertips merely experience the electromagnetic field permeating spacetime, which my brain interprets as, I dunno, this pint glass. The electrons orbiting the nuclei in the glass repel the electrons in the surface of my fingers (like charges repel, if you recall your high school physics), and my brain perceives this unfathomably small gap as texture. Sensory perception is therefore a kind of graphical user interface, like Windows on a PC. We don't perceive atomic structure, just like we don't see the underlying strings of computer code. We see a table, or a chair, or if we're extremely lucky, a timely refill by a convivial barmaid with big tits.

Our sensory organs break down these incoming stimuli into electrical signals, which beam into our brains to be biochemically reassembled into a usable representation. Thus we do actually each exist in our own private illusory Matrix; what we perceive is not reality, it's a biochemical apparition. An hallucination, if you will.**

**I was originally planning to sit back on a porch somewhere to watch the revolution unfold, flicking back popcorn and sipping a choice whisky while the internet pries humanity from its dormant subservience to the hierarchy, but it isn't happening fast enough for my liking. There are cracks in the status quo, though: at the time of writing 23 states of the US have some form of cannabis legalization, and Portugal's policies proves the drug war wrong with everything else. Politicians pay lip service to science when it suits their lust for power, not for accuracy or objectivity. We may have to duct tape them to wooden chairs in abandoned buildings, strap on a few ball gags and erect some kind of movie screen. We'll show them *Tango & Cash* sober, then pump in a pot cloud and reshow it. They'd change the law immediately and hug it out the door.

Anyway, back to the show: Legend has it the 336lb *Stone of Destiny* was used by Jacob (the dad in *Joseph and the Amazing Technicolor Dreamcoat*) as a pillow (probably between songs), and brought to Ireland by the prophet, Bible coauthor (and Obelix prototype?) Jeremiah (who was never in the musical theatre but could apparently carry the fuck out of a rock). It subsequently arrived in Scotland with a wave of 9th century Irish immigrants, who used it as a chair on which to crown their monarchs. It reputedly rested for over four hundred years at Scone Abbey until taken as spoils of war by King Edward I in 1296AD, and whisked away to Westminster Abbey, where it was entombed in their own Coronation Chair. This apparently symbolized the dominion of the English over the Scots, especially if the investing monarch was indulgently flatulent. In 1996, the UK government decided to let Scotland have its fart stone back, and as geologists have proven it to consist of lower old red sandstone quarried just outside Scone (a material which is, topically, immensely permeable to gas), all the stories of its ancient history are, as any reasonable person might have expected, absolute bullshit. (Not that there's anything wrong with a good yarn, but when folks are still prepared to fight and die over what is ostensibly an entertainment, we probably need to soberly reassess the education system. The sooner we get the internet into every pocket on the planet, the better.)

Ancillary fairy tales abound that Edward's prize was, in fact, a fake, while the real Stone of Destiny was prekidnapped for safety by Scottish monks, who bought into this religious nonsense with such zeal they shaved their heads and wore sacks, a worryingly LARPish enthusiasm if ever there was one. But as this mental illness was rampant at the time, judging by the proliferation of elaborate cathedrals, we can probably forgive them their committable befuddlement.

The possibly fake stone was famously stolen back from Westminster Abbey in 1950 by four Scottish students in what was, at first glance, an ingenious Rag Week stunt, until I discovered the act was disappointingly fuelled by that other stunningly insular blight on humanity, nationalism, and from people who should be clever enough, at least on paper, to transcend such simple prejudice. They 'gave it back' to the Scottish nation at Arbroath Abbey, which had some additional parochial meaning, before being recovered and returned to London. No charges were ever brought, which hopefully demonstrates at least a glimmer of humour in the Crown Prosecution Service. I watched a documentary about this on YouTube, where they interviewed one of the now elderly thieves, Ian Hamilton QC (a lawyer of extremely high rank) who actually got emotional about the patriotism of it all. I couldn't help but pity such an utterly lost and myopic old man. His youthful caper should be a celebration of mischief and dissent against the ridiculous. Instead, it was part of the same loopy Harry Potteresque narrative. How sad that someone who lives this long never exercised the opportunity to elevate his perspective. He should go on a bike tour.

Perth is a pleasant-looking city with a fantastic central library, the like more usually found in much larger conurbations. It had a reasonably priced and modern cafe attached, superb WiFi, and no angry wee council rules advocate to admonish me for plugging in.

I sat between two groups who provided such an entertaining day I didn't get a lick of work done. The group to my left were three attractive female students, supposedly working on some assignment, but spending the entire time gossiping with such alacrity I orbited in. They discussed a kaleidoscope of hopes, dreams and motivations, all so stunningly mediocre I was eventually moved by self-importance to intervene.

'Sophia. That's your name? Sophia? Listen, don't believe a word that guy says. Of course he's going to sleep with you and not call you again, you're weird and clingy. Emma: You're a fucking idiot. Don't give advice to anyone ever again. Olivia: you're quite intelligent. It might be time to find more interesting friends than Sophia and Emma. Especially Emma.'

I didn't, of course, because that would be creepy, and continued eavesdropping instead, because that isn't.

The group to my right was a meeting of church goers, three elderly women and one middle-aged man, the man American, midwestern sounding. Two of the women and the man were trying to convince the third woman to join their congregation, which appeared to be some kind of Bible study affair, meeting every Sunday afternoon. The man went on at some length about his philosophy and how it related to scripture, in a rich and soothing baritone, his two supporters cooing at the appropriate moments, obviously enamoured. Was this some kind of senior citizen sex cult recruitment?

The fellow had game. I've heard this kind of patter before, in American topless bars from men trying to 'rescue' the strippers. There's a thin line, as Jimmy Buffett says, between Saturday night and Sunday morning.

After thirty minutes of earnest discussion, the Scottish pensioner they were targeting asked how long their Sunday afternoon Bible studies went on for. The man said it was usually about three hours. She immediately levered herself upright with her walking frame, incensed, '*Three hours*! I don't have time for that! Church all morning then three hours in the afternoon? Are you *insane*?! I've got things to do, goodbye!' She hobbled off, shaking her head and muttering.

There was a moment of awkward silence among the abandoned flock, then the American, lacking even a trace of irony, said, 'I think that went well.'

I Google-mapped a wild hilltop campsite on the outskirts of town and stopped at Morrisons for food on the way, then pitched and watched the moonrise over a landscape blued by the twilight. The stars began to twinkle from the gloom, making me feel very hobbity. I need to get a Churchwarden Briar for times like these. And a better camera.

I did a little reading about Perth that night, and discovered another historical Scottish cannibal called *Christie Cleek*, bringing the total I'd read about to three, and I hadn't even been looking. I haven't mentioned them yet because I didn't think this was a thing, but it was rapidly becoming one. What the hell? Isn't this a little disproportionate for a country of only five million people? I dug around further and discovered Scotland's legacy of serial killers to be a storied one and frankly, a little worrying with me traversing the wild places in a tent. What is wrong with these people?

A Perth butcher called Andrew Christie, in the famine-struck fourteenth century, was driven to roaming the Grampian mountains with a gang in a desperate search for food. A member of his group died, so Christie butchered the body into choice cuts for his fellow gang members. Enthused by this livener, they took to eating travellers and their steeds, Christie using a long shepherd's crook, known as a *Cleke*, hence his sobriquet, to unhorse the victims. Apparently over thirty people were consumed this way before they were apprehended by soldiers from Perth, but Christie apparently escaped and re-entered society under an assumed name, giving rise to his bogeyman status. It's said he died a prosperous merchant in Dumfries many years later.

Christie is often confused with one of the other cannibals I'd read about, but actually pales in comparison to one *Sawyer Bean*. This delightful gourmand headed a forty-eight strong clan of murderous cannibals in the fifteenth or sixteenth century, depending on who you read. Bean lived with his similarly nutter wife in a cave on Bennane Head, a promontory in the Firth of Forth, and, along with his family, preyed on passersby for sustenance. Over several decades they raised fourteen children, who themselves produced, apparently with a little incestuous help from Mom and Pop, thirty-two grandchildren. They were eventually caught and held to be responsible for over 1,000 deaths, and so were executed without trial in Edinburgh. The fathers and brothers were castrated, dismembered and allowed to bleed to death, the women and children burned after watching them die.

We must be delicious.

Back to the library to start a writing assignment I'd picked up yesterday, only to find it closed for staff training, as was the next one along in Kinross. Shit. This little job was time sensitive too, so I decided to roll on for Edinburgh, battling drizzle and a headwind, and camped early just north of Dunfermline in a hilltop forest, because sod drizzle and headwinds.

With time to kill, I threw myself headlong into season two of *Star Trek: The Next Generation.* I've seen all these before, of course, but there's a familiarity to the characters and setting that feels very homey and welcoming. However, after not having seen them for a decade or two, they were looking decidedly dated. Ridiculously so, even. And for a show that purports to demonstrate an absence of prejudice in a future cultural utopia, they certainly have some strong feelings about different alien races, if not human ones. Klingons are a certain way, Vulcans another. Ferengi are a bunch of twats. Gene Roddenberry didn't eradicate prejudice, he disseminated it.

Now, we have a saying in mixed martial arts, 'you have to be the nail before you become the hammer', which alludes to the experience of training. When we first begin, no matter how skilled we may be in our former specialties, be it karate, boxing, wrestling, etc, we always get our arses kicked, because we possess absolute weaknesses in so many other areas, the lack exploited at length by more well-rounded training partners. I hadn't watched TNG since I started training, so I marvelled, from an informed position for the first time, at the Klingon head of security Lieutenant Worf's complete inability to defend himself. Supposedly this highly trained and proud warrior is one to be feared, yet every episode I watched involved him getting smacked about by some alien or other, his bob-cut wig convulsing with impact before he was bodily hurled across the bridge again. Of course, TNG had pretty much ended its run by the time the UFC came around in 1993 and brutally demonstrated how daft the traditional martial arts really are, so we shouldn't judge the Star Trek creators too harshly.

I came to discover there is an actual TV writers' trope nowadays, referred to as *The Worf Effect*, where a known badass, such as Worf, is used as a measuring stick to establish the comparable badassery of an incoming antagonist. When it gets used too often, however, as I witnessed here, a phenomenon occurs known as *Badass Decay*.

Teetering totty totaller Commander Will 'Swinging Dick' Riker, too, was also set up as a badass, but his propensity for using the USS Enterprise as his personal pussy wagon put even legendary intergalactic slut Captain James T. Kirk to shame. Riker cemented this ascendancy by growing a beard when shaving began interfering with bitch banging time.

And I've always been fascinated with the 'beam straight to the bridge' method of capturing unaware characters. What if they're on the toilet? Would they appear on the bridge pants down, mid curl? Would the toilet come too? If not, they're going to fall over. What if the turd shears just before teleportation completed? Would it still transport? Do they even have toilets in Star Trek? Why not just teleport the shit from one's bowels to some waste receptacle? What about leaving it in limbo, looping as a teleporter trace, never to materialize again? If the trace can't be harmlessly dissipated, the atomized data would have to be placed in giant storage drives, hopefully with no download button to accidentally hit (which could undoubtedly make for an entertaining Holodeck malfunction). It's certainly a gaping plot hole, if you'll forgive the expression.

I found a library in Roslyn open until 1pm, then, heading for the Forth road bridge, I bumped into the cycle tourist I lent my spare pump to a few days ago. He was almost home, having just toured Loch Lomond and the Trossachs while I'd been fannying around in Perth. He gave me the pump back then, we wished each other well and I continued on to my old stomping grounds of South Queensferry, where the library was open until five. I watched a stream of England losing 22-30 to New Zealand at Twickenham, and to my horror realized I was wearing my All Black rugby shirt, so it was actually all my fault. I'd like to take this opportunity to apologize to the nation.

I camped at the same spot under the bridge I'd used on my outbound journey, and fell asleep satisfied with the circumnavigation, and dreamed of tomorrow's promised tailwind to Glasgow.

Mist and cobwebs

Twenty years from now you will be more disappointed by the things that you didn't do than by the ones you did do. So throw off the bowlines. Catch the trade winds in your sails. Explore. Dream. Discover. - *Mark Twain*

I flailed through the morning cobwebs and headed south. A couple of minutes later I arrived at the southern terminus of the Forth road bridge and exploited the chance to sit on a 'proper' toilet. I've got to say I wasn't impressed now I'd exorcised the absurdity of the U-bend.

There was an electrical socket by the door, though, so I took the opportunity to prune back my face thicket with my beard trimmer, following up with a good wash. I emerged a shadow of the wildman who'd entered, and bore south towards the bike path that would whisk me to Glasgow.

Over the first hill a low mist hunkered on the valley floor, scattering the morning sunlight pouring over the distant Pentland Hills into an effervescent spectrum of grays. It was insanely beautiful. I could've sat there for hours, but with no problems to ponder, nor passersby to privately ridicule, nor booze to ease the passage of time, being static becomes a little less desirable, and the sunrise would end soon anyway.

If being static is actually even desirable in the first place, as my perspectival iris clicks open to its broader global setting. For example, I did experience an uneasy resistance to leaving the bulkier trappings of civilization behind when I left on this tour, but that resistance existed only in the last week or so of preparation, and lifted, like fuckery bricks from an untended backpack, abruptly upon exiting the driveway. Sudden freedom is surprisingly elating, and seems to eradicate, or at the very least significantly diminish, the petty tribulations of everyday life. Social squabbles and familial friction seem so much less potent, and infinitely more pointless, when one has to procure food and find somewhere to sleep every night.

Therein, perhaps, lies our modern conundrum. We evolved to struggle, not languish in success. With clean water, farmed food, zero predators, permanent shelters, and now the interaction of social media, we can't seem to help but invent new obstacles to take up the emotional slack. Thus, perhaps: neuroses, psychosomatic health irregularities, veganism, melodramatic soap operas, business and exercise goal creation, YouTube comment vitriol, and most curious of them all, plumbing prejudice (some people actually refuse to piss and shit anywhere else but their own home, when even the most rudimentary sanitation protocol dictates the complete opposite). We campaign against animal captivity but seem oblivious to our own. Unfortunately, we've improved healthcare enough to prolong this nightmarish Faustian purgatory into our eighties, when we finally die, peacefully and unnaturally, stuck full of tubes, drugs, and regret, surrounded by sniffling relatives.

A natural death is, of course, being killed by something that wants to eat you. Death by old age in nature is a rare accident, and the terror of mortal pursuit a regular occurrence. We don't have this any more, and we apparently miss its balancing element, because we attempt to fill the void with the facile simulacra of exciting entertainments and precipitous pastimes, and I think this also plays a large part in our indignance at pictorial representations of Mohammad, or the ashes of our national flags, or rape jokes taken out of context. Perhaps we seek the adrenal surf because we're culturally bored, like listless chimps in a concrete zoo? But worse, I reckon, because we blame other chimps rather than the zoo itself.

Maybe I've been hypnotized by the unfurling tarmac, but it seems to be a metaphor for our existence now; a smooth road from the Paleolithic, roughened by overpopulation, potholed by this novel Neolithic concept of property, jolting this old jalopy along to somewhere we never intended to go. Our saving grace may be digital technology, which seems to be bending our road back to a gentler grade, one where we've predominantly evolved to be, and the village is a charming pitstop on the way. And this is the evidence I was seeing, with so many villages now thriving. Twenty years ago they were dying. Hell, maybe village life is as retro as we care to be, now we've sampled the conveniences of indoor plumbing and WiFi routers, and the safety and comfort of the houses we put them in. Hunter-gatherers stay put where food is plentiful, after all. It's the dehumanizing anonymity of towns and cities that do us in.

Personally, I may be taking it a little too far with this modern peripatetic nomadism, but the lifestyle has incredible appeal to me, perhaps because my construction career ran its course, especially in its latter years. In such a physically demanding environment I devalued the common luxuries most of us now take for granted. Plus, as a writer I feel it necessary, if I'm going to write about the way the world is, was, and perhaps will be, to go and have a bloody good look at it.

I followed the old railway track bridleway for most of the day, pondering these hefty topics, and stopped at the Morrisons in Bathgate for a quick forage, coming away with an orgiastically priced 20p bag of toffees.

It started raining mid-afternoon. From the path, I spied a peaceful-looking spot by Hillend Loch, and decided my luck was in. However, traversing a muddy ditch to get to this Eden, I accidentally ripped the heads off my earbuds when one fell out and caught in the front wheel. I did have a backup pair (one of the great advantages of bicycle touring with a trailer: one has more space to build in redundancies), or it would've been tinny phone speaker night in the tent, spiritually destroying the tranquility of the waterside, watching a few more episodes of Riker boldly humping his way through a herd of dead-eyed bimbos and Worf being ragdolled by a smurf.

Hillend Loch is a 345-acre lake created by a dam in 1797. A marvel at the time, it was the largest manmade reservoir in the world. It supplies water to the Forth & Clyde canal, which similarly splits Scotland as the Caledonian canal does, eliminating the need for sea-going vessels to navigate the dangerous waters to the north. The difference between the canals, however, is the Forth & Clyde actually saw a modicum of financial success before being superseded by the railway. Twenty years to build, many thousands of navvies, hundreds of millions of man hours, obsolete twenty years later. It must've been heartbreaking for those callused, determined men.

There is a satisfaction one feels with material work that exceeds any other, I think. I take pride in my writing, so I try to make it as entertaining and fulfilling to read as I possibly can, but the way I feel when I write something well pales in comparison to my satisfaction when I drive past a wall I built or a roof I put on, even twenty or thirty years later. The tangibility is definitely more palpable. So I can empathize with these men when such a monument to their work ethic falls into disuse.

Interestingly, pride is a strange thing, indelibly tied to egotism. I had this conversation recently with one of my best friends, who's an amazing chef, a profession notoriously filled with narcissists, and he took umbrage when I mentioned egotism as a precept for perfectionism. He immediately assumed the layman's interpretation, that ego is infantile, when, in psychological circles, egocentricity is simply a necessary constituent of consciousness. Without it, we lack drive and determination. Much of our motivation stems from this component. I have an ego, as does everyone, but I've learned, especially since beginning to write for a living, to manage it. I want it to drive me towards excellence, but I also require genuine humility when someone purposely disparages me or offers a critique. Then I want to listen and possibly learn by objectively determining the value of the information.

Thus the benefit of balance, so that's now what I strive for, a malleable trade off between pride in my work and the willingness to embrace criticism. Ego is the seed of most strife, but often the solution when applied wisely. Of course, most ill-tempered critics are completely full of shit, but occasionally the target may glean a helpful nugget from the avalanche of bile.

The winter had apparently followed me down from the mountains, as the flysheet was frozen this morning, but the low sun quickly defrosted tent, bike tarp, and the long grass around me, creating a damp mist that ultimately drenched everything. It dissipated quickly enough, though, and dried things out before I packed up.

Petersburn library on the outskirts of Glasgow appeared to be a relic of Assault on Precinct 13, a concrete bunker with tiny barred windows, flanked by shuttered shops defaced by graffiti, on a tower block housing estate replete with the rooster-like strutting of pit bull advocates manfully reining in their pet predators. The librarian eyed me nervously from behind his bulwark desk as I walked in. I tried the wandering writer rhetoric, and relief washed over the man like a papal benediction. So thankful I wasn't there to violently bugger him to death he offered me access to the internet via his own account when the guest system went down. The place was deserted, and no other customer came in the library for the two hours I was there, which somehow didn't surprise me, though another librarian did turn up and they discussed me in hushed, almost reverential tones which had the curious effect of not only buffing my ego but also worrying me about my rig locked outside. I finished my final draft, emailed it to the client, landed another little project, then left to skirt the periphery of Glasgow and head south for the border and Carlisle.

I camped by Strathclyde Loch between Hamilton and Motherwell, near Bothwellhaugh Roman ruins (which destroy the popular Scottish boast of the empire ending at Hadrian's Wall some eighty miles to the south), and next to a suspiciously sandy beach, made the single most momentous discovery in the history of cycle touring: No Bake Camp Cheesecake. You take a digestive cookie, break it in half to make it bite-sized and surmount each with a generous dollop of cream cheese, then a slight smear of bramble jelly. With a succession of cups of tea, I was in heaven. Surely something this divinely simple had been invented before? Well, I'm taking credit for it even if it has, because by gum, the symphony of sweet, oaty crunch, smooth creamy cheese and sharp tang of berry is to die for, especially augmented by an eruptive lakeside sunset.

After weeks of cycling spending more and more of my time not listening to anything and becoming something of a meditative hippie, I curiously found myself craving music upon discovering my backup earbuds had even less purchase in my ears than the previous pair. I spent morning tent defrosting time loading up a new rockin' playlist to my phone and hit the road with the rolled frozen flysheet strapped to the trailer because it hadn't.

I rode to Larkhall to work and charge my phone in the library, and discovered I'd been paid promptly for the work I sent in yesterday. I completed today's assignment and headed for the Co-op for an indulgent shop of curry ingredients and a celebratory four pack, thinking to get a couple of more hours riding in and camp early for dinner and a movie. This plan evaporated, however, when an elderly 'I'm Scottish' American cornered me as I was unlocking my bike and subjected me to a litany of family migratory history, mistaking my Canadian cycling jersey for collusion.

Coming from Britain, as I do (though born in Canada), I've never understood the North American fascination with their European ancestry. The stereotyping underpinning such interest is often quite disturbing, and rather shocking to experience from the denizens of First World countries, who should, frankly, know better. European nobility have the same obsession, and normal people shouldn't trust those weird bastards either.

Perhaps it's a relic from when we thought lineage and geography were more important than the individual, and we didn't know enough about humanity to discard the proverbial book cover? After all, this was before the internet, and I suppose the quickest way to best guess someone's character and temperament was through the generous application of established stereotypes. We weren't to know such thinking was lazy horseshit. It shocks me to see how many people still harbour these views, expressed so easily within the anonymity of the web, even with the mountains of biological evidence stacked so heavily against them and freely available for all to see. But still, this guy was ancient, so the stratifications of prejudice were probably irrevocably ingrained.

Avoiding impoliteness I murmured platitudes and feigned interest at the appropriate points, whilst internally updating how far I'd be able to ride now before darkness hit. When he finally broke the monologue at the sixty minute mark to draw what I firmly believe was his first breath, I interrupted to say I had to get going, constructing some lie about having to be in Carlisle in two days, and it was 120K away. He dismissed my objections and grabbed my arm, offering me a bed for the night. An entire evening of subjective genealogy, accompanied, no doubt, by albums of pictorial evidence, bookcases of supporting literature, slide shows, laser-pointed Powerpoint presentations, and, quite possibly, surreptitious attempts at sado-masochistic sex. I thanked him but refused, and said I really had to leave.

I was probably a little brusque in declining, and hope I didn't hurt his feelings, as he was probably just a lonely old man looking for someone to talk to, but I'd already given him an hour and I was looking forward to my plans. Curry night!

I made a mad scramble out of town before the dark and cold hit, desperate to find a place to camp. I finally found a fair spot and discovered my flysheet was still frozen. I put the beer outside to chill and slow cooked the curry for a couple of hours, seriously denting my methylated spirits supply but man, was it worth it for both my sanity and the sanctity of my bottom.

The old Carlisle road paralleling the M74 was virtually deserted. I saw two cars in twenty miles, and with a dedicated bike path and a healthy tailwind through hilly terrain, I did that twenty miles in about ninety minutes. With the sun out and great views, the euphoria rose to a point where I started singing along to the music I was listening to, especially when Big Joe Turner came on with his version of the classic Honey Hush. I particularly like the chorus, so was belting it out at the top of my lungs, 'I SAID A-HI HO, HI HO SILVER! HI HO SILVER AWAAAAYYY!' when I shot out from the forest track, on a black bike, no less, onto a footway in front of two startled backpackers.

I passed through the village of Abington, but neglected to turn off for Wanlockhead, the highest village in Scotland at 1,531' (467 m) above sea level and home to what is very probably an interesting lead mining museum, but it would be closed for the winter. I continued on and noticed, on a bare hillside to my left, a patch of pine forest, just outside

Crawford, quite blatantly planted in the shape of a giant penis. Immensely amused, pictures immediately winged their way to my Twitter and Facebook accounts.

I rode on past the rapturously named villages of Elvanfoot and Watermeetings, tyres purring their approval in the silence, but this perfect day began to crumble with the simplicity of missing a turn. Not usually a big deal, but I didn't notice I had, and this turn was important: it crossed the motorway to continue the trail on the other side of the valley. Sleet began to fall and blow sideways. The tarmac gave way to a dirt track, the track thence to mud, and there was nowhere to camp. I saw some woods up ahead, though, and slogged on into them, thinking I was still on the right route, to discover a gate blocking my path. It was some kind of quarrying or mining operation, so I checked my map and discovered where I'd gone wrong. Still there was nowhere to pitch, so I donned waterproofs and backtracked the couple of miles through the mud slurry, now washing away to expose rough stone aggregate necessitating a snail's pace lest my rig shudder apart, the headwind opposing smoother stretches, as I cursed the heavens and all they contain.

I made it back to the missed junction, the cold starting to bite, got on the right path, cranked up my cadence to warm up, and discovered my trailer tyre was flat. I couldn't help but chuckle at how not fun this was. I pumped the thing up and carried on. It lasted perhaps a hundred yards. My hands were too numb to fix the puncture and it was getting dark and colder, one side of the road was a bog, the other fenced off, which isn't particularly a problem for me, but the dense and steeply sloping forest beyond was. I pumped up again, repeating the routine three times until I came across a flatter area to the left, raised above the bog.

In the dark I pitched on mossy rubble over concrete, trying to find purchase with the pegs, as the winter wind whirled into a howl. My hands had no feeling anyway, so I degloved to defrost them in armpits or crotch for half a minute to open up a few seconds of fiddling with pegs, zips, and clasps. It was below freezing now, and the sky was clearing to reveal gimlet stars, the moon an indifferent chip of ice, so removed from civilization's glow. It was going to get even colder. I spread my stuff inside, weighting the corners to augment the insecure pegs, and thankfully, finally, got out of the elements.

I discovered, to my dismay, that my sleeping bag was wet. This was going to be interesting, as it's a two season bag with a comfort rating of +2 degrees Celsius and an Extreme Rating of -3, and it was already about -5 C, I guestimated*. Extreme Rating means you'll probably survive that temperature, but you won't sleep. I did have a silk liner though, which makes a huge difference, and I could layer up my clothing, but I was out of candles for the heater. There are those who say one should sleep naked or only in very light clothing in order to extract the full benefit of a sleeping bag. I don't believe these people.

I still woke up shivering and unable to feel my bare feet (all my socks were also wet), the tent taking a serious beating from the wind. I went out several times to adjust the guys and pegs, and actually wrote in my notes, 'HOLY FUCKING JESUS IT'S COLD!!!' when I got back in, but all told I was pretty comfortable, considering. Especially when I used my headover and woolly hat as socks instead, and wore two pairs of spare underpants on my head, and spread my towel over the bottom of my bag as a blanket. The benefit of so many years working construction in Canadian winters and Texan summers is I'm intimately familiar with a hell of a lot worse than this.

*I'm pretty good at marking temperatures. I looked at the weather report the next morning, and it had reached -6 C, so I was pretty close.

Kicking down walls in the north of England

For the first time in my life, I can truly say, without any nagging internal caveat, that I've never been happier. And I think it's because I'm finally doing something to assuage my innate wanderlust; a natural consequence, I believe, of our overwhelmingly nomadic ancestry. I've mentioned before how the homo genus has only been static for the last 0.4% of our time on Earth: 99.6% of our 2.5 million years or so were spent as hunter-gatherers, so I think it's fairly logical to assume we're driven by our genes to ford the river and climb the mountain. Ignoring this deeply ingrained predisposition is one of the main causes of our everyday stress, I believe, and a supreme cosmic irresponsibility, if one ponders the pot brownie idea that consciousness could well be the universe's attempt to understand itself. I think the recreation we feel when we hit the beach, the woods, or the slopes is precisely that mechanism kicking into gear, emerging like a sharp sword from a timeworn scabbard, tattered by a decamillennium of neglect. Movement is truly what we're born to do; material acquisition is a recent invention, because stuff just weighs us down.

In the modern world, all this changes when you involve someone else, of course. Success attracts mates, and finery is the easiest way to show it off, so it becomes expected, and an end in itself. But finery is an empty goal. Life is about experience, because that's all we take with us. After all, what do we reminisce about? Jewelry? Cars? Big screen TVs? Of course not. It's the howls of laughter, the tender amity, and the shared adventure. Our real goal, once we learn to transcend the cultural bullshit, is to fill our lives with unique and meaningful moments, because these are the only things that really matter.

At least, that's the theory. When it comes to happiness in relationships, I've had girlfriends ask me to change many seemingly innocuous behaviours in order to facilitate theirs. Aside from the usual toothpaste and toilet seat battles, one particularly memorable one was to make sure all the light switches on the main multi-switch panel in our open plan apartment were always facing the same direction by daily traipsing around 1,400 square feet coordinating their ancillaries. I flatly refused, which, curiously and gratefully, catalyzed our breakup. I've been asked to change more overt behaviours, too, such as playing sports or socializing with friends. Now, perhaps they didn't realize these things make *me* happy, or simply didn't care? Or maybe I was being too selfish?

Either way, if one's partner's happiness correlates with the other's wretchedness, as it certainly seems to have with a significant number of my relationships, I think it may be prudent to ditch the partner rather than adopt their light switch neuroses. This lack of compromise may strike some people as petty, but I've always preferred my own company over the abject misery of throw pillows and ironed underwear.

Whenever I get into a relationship, the first three months are fantastic, but then I seem to gradually lose interest. I don't become bored, per se, but lacklustre, ready to move on, only sticking around because I'm expected to. Because of this, I've never had a relationship last beyond a couple of years, and they all typically followed the same pattern of three months of joy followed by twenty-odd months of loyalty (well, I am stubborn). I thought I was broken, so I looked for solutions to this anti-monogamy trend. It turns out I'm no more broken than anyone else; they're just willing to put up with it. (I've heard it theorized that men are naturally tuned to stray after about three to four months, because that's when a pregnancy begins to show—job done—but I've never seen, or even looked for, any empirical evidence to support the idea. This doesn't mean it might not be true, however.)

It took me a couple of decades bouncing from one girl to another to realize this: all compromise ever got me was mediocrity; a halfway house of temporarily acceptable agreeableness in which neither party is truly happy, and, with my rapidly justifying fickleness firing on all cylinders, ultimately dooming the relationship. Most married couples (or 50–60% of them, anyway, depending on which divorce statistic you read) seem willing to struggle on through a lifetime, evinced by the bitter squabbles of the long-married, soured by missed opportunities and enlivened by the chance to twist the knife over a past transgression, simply to perpetuate, it seems to me, the convenience of a regular shag. Have you ever met an old married couple who didn't constantly run each other down? In my experience, they seem to be the exception rather than the rule.

I suggest we shouldn't compromise. We should do what we like, and if a partnership evolves from connections made organically, great. If it doesn't, great too, because one is still doing exactly what one wants to do. A relationship shouldn't take work, I now believe, despite the popular rhetoric to the contrary. Do you have to work at your relationship with your best friends? I hope you said 'no', because if you all do, I'm either supremely easy to get along with or a complete sociopath.

This all stems, of course, from that monumental bugbear of modern humanity: monogamy. We're not naturally monogamous, as any objective anthropologist or psychologist will tell you (a good primer on this is Dr.

Christopher Ryan's book *Sex at Dawn*). Monogamy came about (as far as I can tell, after sifting through the absolute mountains of evidence pointing to polyamory as our true nature) with the Neolithic concept of property and advent of organized religion, no doubt adopted to systemize human breeding for maximum yield to fill the fields, armies, and factories on which the hierarchy of this abrupt cultural aberration so vitally depends. Monogamy means more children per woman, which means more food for the machine: drones, if you will, and plenty of them.

So we're naturally, happily, polyamorous, because we've spent almost our entire history being so. Our psychological architecture evolved this way, but we're now stuck in this mad monogamous game of sexual exclusivity because it serves the state. And somehow we've managed to convince ourselves, through subservience to puritanical religions, that there's morality involved; a lingering deception of such magnitude and pervasiveness one can but both marvel and despair.

To quote neuroscientist and author Sam Harris, who puts this far more competently than I:

The God that our neighbors /*sic*/ believe in is essentially an invisible person. He's a creator deity, who created the universe to have a relationship with one species of primates – lucky us. And he's got galaxy upon galaxy to attend to, but he's especially concerned with what we do, and he's especially concerned with what we do while naked. He almost certainly disapproves of homosexuality. And he's created this cosmos as a vast laboratory in which to test our powers of credulity, and the test is this: can you believe in this God on bad evidence, which is to say, on faith? And if you can, you will win an eternity of happiness after you die.

Men have told me at dinner parties, typically in front of a hawkish wife similarly sold on the social propaganda, about how rapturous they are in this exclusive monogamy; usually men who feel the need to champion the fairer gender so long held to be property by agrarian civilizations. I like to answer by asking the men if the only porn they watch when they masturbate is of their wife, and similarly, do their wives only read romance novels and watch soap operas (obstinately perpetuating these particularly entrenched stereotypes) about their relationship with their husband? This sometimes produces an uneasy silence, depending on how stuck up the company is, not just because it's an awkward situation to consider (masturbation is rarely a topic addressed in polite society, which is one of the many reasons polite society is so suicidally fucking tedious) but also because they're stumped, if you'll pardon the expression.

The response I enjoy the most, however, is the haughty 'we don't need to masturbate' routine, because everybody listening knows this to be the kind of colossal whopper usually reserved for and by priests, politicians and toddlers. The typical layperson doesn't know, of course, comparatively little research has been done on masturbation, simply because finding subjects who refrain from fiddling with themselves to fill control groups is so goddamned difficult. People wank. Those who say they don't are lying. And, as a *hedono-anarcho-primito-apocaloptimist*, I think denying oneself harmless, private, nurturant pleasure is child molester weird; the 'moral' objection to it is simply another social remnant of the state optimizing breeding turnover by doctrinal manipulation. If people think eternal damnation awaits those who masturbate, they're going to try harder to get laid. And I don't think I'm alone.

Well, I am, but you know what I mean.

I hope.

Yeah, last night sucked. I managed to get a little sleep despite the cold, and woke to a sunny but frigid mountain world.

I quickly fixed the flat on my trailer, but noticed the tyre itself was blown through, a hole about an inch across as if made by a sharp rock, probably from riding the rubble road yesterday. I patched it with a piece of old inner tube specifically reserved for this purpose, and hoped it would hold me the hundred miles home.

A welcome tailwind powered me along: I was easily going to make Carlisle today, until I got another puncture on my front tyre, which turned out to be two thorns, each of them having made two holes, which took me all morning and about half a mile to figure out (this is when I suddenly remembered the importance of checking the tyre before reinserting the inner tube). With sunlight only available between about 9 am and 3.30 pm this far north so late in the autumn, I only had around four hours of riding a day, bookended by camp prep and break. So I only actually made around 25 miles when I was shooting for 40, and ended up camping at Lockerbie.

I got a curious email from my mother asking if I want to be rescued from the rapidly approaching winter. Bless her cotton socks. I don't know if such naïveté springs from my reluctance to share the particulars of my life with my parents (in order to avoid their unrelenting disapproval), or from her stunning lack of faith in her son's ability to deal with, what she seems to perceive as, hardship.

In this latter perception she's not alone. The sheer number of people who've expressed awe in what I'm doing is quite overwhelming, as if it's some great physical and spiritual trial. Let me tell you right now: it isn't. Every day on tour is an adventure, sure, packed with novelty, but in no way is it 'hard'. Hardship is monotonously doing the same thing every day, commuting from a cookie cutter house to a cookie cutter cubicle, or fighting in a war, or summer roofing in Texas, or concreting anytime anywhere, in order to chip away at some tectonic debt. It certainly isn't cycling from pub to pub looking at cool shit along the way. This is easy. The problem isn't physicality or loneliness; it's maintaining enough of a positive revenue stream to continue with equipment upkeep and food. Because shit breaks, a lot. When you consider the planned obsolescence of most camping and cycling products are for a few weekends a year, I'm asking rather more of my gear. So it's no wonder everything is fraying, creaking and snapping. I notice the most expensive stuff is more hardwearing, which sucks, because I don't particularly want to spend more money than I have to. However, it looks like I may have to plonk down some serious coin over the next few months for equipment I consider unnecessarily dear. I tend to be of the mindset of not carrying anything I'm not prepared to lose, and the more I spend, the more this mood diminishes.

A slow flat got worse on my front tyre and required pumping up three or four times today, as slow punctures are difficult to find without immersing the inner in water, and messing about with a collapsible bucket of water in freezing temperatures is firmly in 'fuck that' territory. I noticed my trailer tyre was slowly deflating too, but it got me to Carlisle where a slippery data connection meant I asked directions to the library, and was sent down the wrong street. Luckily, it was a crowded pedestrian precinct so I dismounted and pushed, allowing the rather overweight fellow who'd misdirected me to catch up once he'd realized the error, at a full, red-faced, lung-bursting sprint.

These altruistic demonstrations help confirm my suspicions that the majority of us are inherently nice. On bicycle tours we get exposed to so many people without the physical barriers of road traffic, or the psychological ones we erect on public transport or in travel hubs, so one experiences a much broader yet concentrated form of human interaction. Plus, the bike seems to strip the pretense from social conditioning: there's no way to judge the rider's affluence, so people are forced to dig for further cues, and most of us, I think, with the internet sounding the death knell of the class system, can no longer be bothered with such juvenile juxtapositioning.

The WiFi in the library wasn't working, so the librarian generously allowed me an hour on one of the public computers which normally require some kind of fee, and made it clear she didn't do this for just anyone, y'know. This simultaneously separated me from the imaginary hordes of riff raff who roam from library to library to con local councils out of free online time, and established her position as a middle class chauvinist, no doubt trusting that my cycling jersey, by now specifically worn to elicit this very response, superceded every other indicator of grubby proletarianism. Yeah, so I'm a social climber.

I worked until the library closed at 5.30pm, and I made my way through the unfamiliar city in the dark, to Rickerby Park to camp, and pitched by head torch next to a footbridge over the River Eden, desperately hoping this wasn't where the drug addict, axe murderer, and cottaging communities held their weekly knees up.

This was the best 'make camp in the dark' result yet. I woke sober, alive and unbuggered, and waited for the sky to grey before rising to a pretty parkland scene by the river.

It was -2 degrees Celsius, so I packed up quickly and hit the road to warm up. I headed east, riding mostly uphill into the Pennines, arriving in Brampton before lunch.

Brampton is a fetching little village with a tiny library and an accommodating librarian, who signed me into a computer on her account when we similarly couldn't get the WiFi to work. It was a Saturday, so when it closed at 1 pm I headed higher into the mountains, following the course of Hadrian's Wall, and spent the night in its shadow at Walltown Quarry picnic site, contemplating the brutal life of a Roman soldier at the edge of the ancient world.

Overnighting here is probably especially illegal, but by this point I was so past caring about arbitrary camping laws invented by people who don't camp I was quite prepared to bury the violently strangled agent of any objectionable officialdom with my toilet trowel.

To entertain myself over the usual episodes of *Star Trek: The Next Generation*, I came up with the concept of the *Limited Nutritional Value Pig Out Night*. On the menu were two packets of Rich Tea biscuits, two packets of Digestives, a jar of smooth peanut butter, a jar of jam, a tub of cream cheese and unlimited cups of tea. Which, let's be honest here, is what this bicycle touring malarkey is *really* all about.

Tim and me

For me, meeting Tim Ferriss was a life changer. Not because he's a particularly inspirational individual (he is), nor because he's wildly successful (he is), but because it was his lifestyle I eventually decided to pursue. Well, not his *actual* lifestyle; my *perception* of his lifestyle.

We met in 2010. I was hired to interview him for the blog of a freelance contracting platform called Elance.com I used while starting out as a professional writer, and I had no idea who he was.

Elance.com is also the company, incidentally, who launched a $10,000 essay competition in 2009 about their tagline concept *The New Way to Work*. Here was my effort:

Let's face it. I'm lazy.

I have a job bookended by twenty foot commutes. I can execute my professional duties wearing a Snuggie™ and fluffy bunny bedroom slippers. I shave when the mood strikes me. Whim dictates my breaks. I vacation when I please. These freedoms fill me with the profound, emotional joy usually reserved for the birth of offspring or three-pointing a crumpled ball of paper on the first go.

As I recline in my contoured office chair at

my unnecessarily large desk, surrounded by bright computer screens, stocked bookshelves, and the detritus of errant free-throw attempts, I find it difficult to avoid aiming a glimmer of smugness at you poor buggers who actually have to work for a living. Because what I do is not work; at least not in the traditional sense. I get paid to play with words. People are actually quite prepared to give me money for this rubbish, which never ceases to boggle my noggin.

Laziness, you see, is not necessarily a fault. Every device, every invention, every idea came into being because someone was looking for an easier way to get something done. Laziness prompts us to perform more quickly and efficiently, so we can increase our time in its pursuit. It is the cyclical human condition.

Now consider the rarefied word that describes what I do: freelance. To me, it conjures up the image of a laconic lone wolf, a similarly unshaven man with no name, if you will, slowly striding the dusty streets of commerce selling his deadly services to whomever will pay.

This iconic avatar is not, may I point out, shuffling along in a light blue onesie. And spurs don't jingle quite so menacingly, I imagine, while buried deeply in soft bunny fluff. His slugs of rotgut whiskey and well-chewed cheroot have been usurped in reality by mugs of comforting cocoa and, if I'm feeling particularly dangerous, a chocolate cookie.

My mouse is my gun, my prose ammunition. At the risk of overtaxing this metaphor's tensile elasticity, I will forgo spuriously likening Elance.com to Eli Wallach by inelegantly linking their first two letters. Instead, I will mention the days of frantically scouring trade publications and the like for potential clients are forever over. Now they come to me, delivered via Elance's colossal online fish-barrel. It's almost criminally easy. See, in the bad old days, freelance writing was an analogue profession. We had to roam the figurative tundra in search of paying work. We had to proactively make phone calls and traipse to libraries to conduct our research. Paper was occasionally used for projects more productive than wastebasketball. Effort was actually a requirement of the vocation. Then, some bright (but lazy) spark invented the internet. This begat Elance.com, which begat a burgeoning industry of workers who clumsily slop milk-sodden Fruit Loops down their pajama fronts with the indifference of an untended infant.

I'm not sure this is what Elance anticipated when they envisioned The New Way to Work. Personally, I don't mind if clients erroneously believe I'm a facsimile of the blustery editor in a high-pressure broadsheet newsroom, all rolled-up shirt-sleeves and furiously masticated pencils, fingers gradually typing less madly as the caffeine-fuelled hustle is delicately redressed by Liquid Paper fumes. After all, who am I to derail their delusion? Obviously, Elance planned to accrue an exhaustive index of such hard-boiled archetypes. However, instead (and I'm sure to their everlasting horror) they got people like me.

By rights, working from home should have exploded when the internet arrived. There's no real reason for people to physically travel to an office building anymore. Email, instant messaging, cell phones, video conferencing, pervasive WiFi and online workrooms should have euthanized the archaic concept of the communal administrative workplace, but they haven't yet. Why is this?

Could it possibly be the people who own large businesses are oblivious to the motivational aspects of our quest for idleness? Do they firmly believe their lazy employees require robust, adjacent, slave galley-like supervision? A bleak observation, granted, but what other reason could there be? I've posed this question to colleagues who espouse this paradigm. They invariably answer: "Meetings are more effective in person." That may be, but does one really require special premises (and all the expense they entail) for something so mundane? If you feel the need to get tangible when you talk about work, can you not sit down for a chinwag at your house? You know there are pubs, clubs, restaurants, hotels, malls, convention centers, churches, temples and coffee shops with meeting rooms, right?

I'm willing to bet most people who advocate formal, nay, ceremonial meetings in office surroundings do so because it buffs their self-importance to walk into an engagement sporting a Savile Row pinstripe, an Underwood briefcase and a Scott Tracey haircut: the comical, outmoded trappings of modern "power". Negotiate from a position of perceived strength is the applicable adage here, I believe, even if that strength is umbilically tied to the truncated fashions of a 1960s children's puppet show. I think it taps the same conceit originally evolved by the caveman carrying the prettiest club into the forest: Me best hunter.

As far as I can ascertain, a far more accurate contemporary summation would be; Me dunno how to work them internets. It's time to rid the village of this hirsute knuckledragger, folks. Pompous, contentless, physical formality in business is dying, as well it should. We may as well drag it behind the shed and put it out of its misery.

Writing this reminds me of something I said

fifteen years ago. I was walking through Central Park with my girlfriend, marveling at the surrounding skyscrapers. The internet was first really starting to take off. "See these wonderful office buildings? They'll all be fancy apartments in five years," I predicted. "No business in its right mind will run things from such expensive central locations when there's online offices. Everyone will be working from home. You watch."

Yeah, so I was wrong.

But that watch is ticking.

Not bad, right? I was quite proud of it as a piece of writing, but it didn't even place in the top ten! The winners won with, by comparison, an enthusiastically sloppy bout of corporate fellatio. '*They have no art!*' I roared in my new career naivety.

Tim and I were scheduled to meet at one of his book signings for the *Four Hour Work Week*, which obviously I hadn't read, as coming straight from a construction background and never having worked in an office environment, I'd had absolutely no exposure to the flimsy-wristed onanism of self-help literature. I got to the location and figured it might be an idea to read the thing before I talked to him, so I grabbed a copy and flicked through it for an hour. I read fast, so I got the gist.

The subsequent interview wasn't an interview at all, really, because I was a little drunk. It was party day at the SXSW Interactive Conference in Austin, Texas, (which is where this book signing was taking place), and all the stalls were manically pushing free booze. This means I'd had many beverages unceremoniously thrust at me as I meandered through the nerd maze, waiting for Tim to finish signing, and such was his popularity the event ran over by four hours. Thus the hall was swaying like a maritime mistake when we finally sat down to talk. We got along famously, of course, as when I'm pissed I'm tremendously gregarious, and we share a common interest in mixed martial arts, which we discussed at some length to the distress of my far more professional interview partner Brittany. Brittany dutifully punctuated the exuberant babble with proper questions and recorded the conversation on her iPhone, all the while staring in horror at my inappropriate familiarity with the great man.

Behind the boundless vulgarity and exuberance I tried to figure out who Tim was, because there wasn't a page for him in my mental archetype Rolodex. Was he really a nomadic worker, travelling the world working four hours a week online? Did he have any kind of static base to work from? Did he own a house, for example? Rent an apartment? It turned out Tim lived a lot more of a conventional life than the impression I got from his book, but it's the life I'd *imagined* I found compelling. (Sorry Tim. I'm pretty sure your real life is awesome, but not, apparently, as much as it could be). I decided right there and then, I wanted that. Not what Tim does, but what I *thought* he does; travelling and working on the road. Obviously, I had no idea it would take many years and cost tens of thousands of dollars to get myself into a position to do so, to extricate myself from the complex prison we call western life, and henceforth embark on an incremental change in my fundamental philosophies, but the seed had been planted, and planted deep.

Travelling solo, I find I begin to conform to my personal ideals, like I'm the protagonist of my own novel, probably because they're the most available benchmarks to go by. But on returning, if I spend any significant time reintegrating with family and friends, I begin to slowly conform to their expectations of the way I used to be: the walls of the familiar loom and creep closer. And this is undesirable, especially when you don't particularly like who, or perhaps more accurately where, you used to be. When people expect me to be a certain way, I seem to follow the path of least resistance, which is to gradually drift back to their point of view. This destroys any progress one's made, and, especially if one's aware of it, even subconsciously, can lead to a listless depression.

Everybody changes over time: otherwise, they're wasting it. We learn and grow as we plod through life, but travelling accelerates this process to a sprint. A few short months can have a profound effect on the way we view the world and interact with people. The ability to broaden our perspective is an immensely valuable tool, directly proportional to the miles we cover, unavailable to those chained to a mortgage. The *way* we travel, too, is important. Some of my elderly relatives and friends spring to mind: they overemphasize cultural differences like many of their generation, completely comfortable with racist rhetoric, oblivious to the global social revolution heralded by the internet, which they view as some kind of idiot novelty, like flared trousers or head boppers, but get dragged along on exotic retirement trips by their significant others. Do they appreciate the history and vibrant cultures of the far flung places they visit? Nope. They like how many desserts one can have in the all-U-can-eat cruise ship restaurant, or how far the US dollar and British pound stretch in third world countries, or the novelty of a British pub interior with a Mediterranean patio. I believe this to be a result of the detachment encouraged by speedy transport. If they had to power themselves to these places they'd learn to appreciate the journey, and I'm sure they'd have trouble maintaining such prejudicial opinions about the people. It's difficult to maintain an exclusionary political stance when one's part of the reason drowned toddlers wash ashore.

Look, we're homogenizing anyway. Communication causes cultures to merge: it's what it's ultimately *for*, and with the internet, the cat is well and truly out of the bag. No amount of politicking is going to tease it back in, and damage control by the powers that be just delay things. Their day is over. We're heading for global government with online voting and far fewer professional politicians, so fuck countries. Let's get on with it. Countries were a stupid idea in the first place and are actually holding us back: whether they're a Mesolithic misstep that got away from us or a necessary middle act to a greater way of being, they're transitory. I say we head towards, or circumnavigate back to, who we actually evolved to be, if our evidence of an overwhelming number of Paleolithic cultures is anything to go by: reasonable, communicative, egalitarian, and happy.

I decided on a more direct route home (because my mate in Newcastle turned out to be in Spain, a sign I should prepare further ahead) via Haltwhistle (love that name, plus it's the geographic centre of Great Britain, according to the midpoint of compass lines) then on to Alston and across the Pennines. The roads were quiet with a lot of climbing, but I found a cadence to match the steady incline and musicked up to make it fun. The snow on the tops made me feel adventurous, and the temperatures were noticeably cooler, but the cycling kept me warm, and the clear views wholesome. I passed several snowbound farmhouses, so far from anywhere, which made me a little jealous, before the downhill that changed my life.

Most people in Britain are familiar with the beauty of the Yorkshire Dales, thanks largely to the books by James Herriot popularizing the place, but they have no idea the same landscape occurs a little to the north in Northumberland, and with far fewer people. It is exquisitely gorgeous, especially with the snow dusting the tips. The sun greeted my downhill like an old mate, and the road, again, was freshly surfaced thanks to Northumberland's bid for the opening stage of the Tour de France that year. So there was no tyre noise, and no traffic, and no people, just me and the world. *Travelgasm* #3.

About halfway down to Middleton-upon-Tees, I passed a proper cyclist taking on water after his daily climb. He'd hit his high point, turned around, caught me up, and we chatted all the way into the village. I told him about exploring the UK to see how villages were faring, but he disagreed with my premise. He said technology is killing communication, whereas I think it enlivens it. It was interesting to hear a rural opinion, however, as he lambasted city immigrants to the country, who apparently refuse to integrate with the local community as much as he'd like. 'They don't come in the pub', was his particular chagrin. And fair point, I think: if you live in a village and don't frequent the pub, you've got to be some kind of twat.

I camped on the other side of Middleton and cursed my plastic mug again for being too small: it was such a pain boiling eight fluid ounces of water when I prefer to drink coffee by the pint. That's when the brainwave hit: why not boil a litre at a time and make the coffee in my one litre food thermos? It had a handle, so could be used as a huge mug. Displeased this had only taken me two, often bitterly cold, months to figure out, I decided to enjoy the anticipation of copious coffee on my last two nights rather than bash myself over the head with it shouting 'Stupid! Stupid! Stupid!'

Turning over in a mummy sleeping bag requires significant forethought and logistical acumen. The detachable inner must be kept in concert with the bag or the occupant often ends up in a litany of twisted WWII Japanese prison camp stress positions. Thus I woke with a strangled gurgle at 4.30 this morning. I strategically struggled free and grabbed the empty methylated spirits bottle reserved specifically for pissing purposes: it saves messing with shoes, tent flaps and cold air rushing into my snug cocoon. After relieving myself I unzipped the tent door to empty the bottle, and the sound in the still mountain air carried to the nearest farm, about a quarter of a mile distant. This woke the dog, if the sudden barking was anything to go by. Barking subsequently started at another farm about half a mile from there, and so on down the valley in a cacophonous relay, closely trailed by a procession of angrily illuminating windows, the Teesdale Canine Telegraph presaging a sight not unlike Gondor's desperate call to Rohan. It was an impressive sight. Envisioning gnarled farming hands reaching for bedside shotguns, I quickly poured out the contents and retreated to the twisted seclusion of my sleeping bag, wondering if any relocated townies were now cursing their romantic notions of living in the outback.

The sunrise that morning was probably lost on the grim and bleary-eyed locals, but I enjoyed it immensely as it drenched the autumnal colours in reds and golds. It's difficult to believe just a few short miles down the valley this sublime sight would give way to the urban horror of Stockton-on-Tees.

I quickly shivered into my sweat-frozen cycling gear and set off for

Barnard Castle by way of the Church of St Romald in Romaldkirk, a
Norman affair known rather ambitiously as the 'Cathedral of the Dales', with
sections dating back to Saxon times. The village was destroyed a couple of
times by invading Scots in the 14th century, but the residents stoically rebuilt
into the fine example of a prosperous 18th century village it remains today.

The town of Barnard Castle centres on a magnificent namesake ruin, and
has to be one of the most pleasant-looking towns I visited. I dismounted to
walk up a castleside path into the town proper, escorted by an elderly
strolling ex-solider, who quizzed me about my journey, and as usual the
conversation turned to security. What the hell is everyone so frightened of?
Did they know something I didn't? Were there monsters out there? I was
starting to feel like some lost, wandering soul in The Walking Dead.

I arrived at the library to discover no WiFi and no charging facilities.
With waning batteries I booked one of their computers for half an hour,
frantically Google mapped directions and wrote them down with a pen and
paper. I left not a little annoyed with Barnard Castle Council customer
service policies, and set off down the A66 for Scotch Corner. This proved to
be a drastic and near fatal mistake. While the shoulder was a couple of feet
wide for a few miles, it suddenly disappeared, leaving a very narrow two
lane road dominated by massive HGV traffic thundering past at sixty miles
per hour, sometimes literally within inches. It was fucking terrifying, I don't
mind admitting. I only had to endure about half a mile to the next turn off,
but that 800 yards left me shaking.

Some people wonder why I don't turn back in these situations. Often you
can't tell how dangerous a stretch of road is going to be until you're already
too far along to consider backtracking. In this particular situation, navigating
by a single route on a piece of paper (thanks, Barnard Castle Council) I had

no option other than get totally lost, and backtracking to the two foot shoulder would've been just as deadly once I was halfway to the turnoff, and turning around itself would've been even more dangerous.

Back in safety my trailer tyre blew again in the same place, the tear growing to an inch across. I repaired it with another section of inner tube as best I could. It held for another five or six miles until the dark forced me to camp on an old country estate behind a derelict house. I resolved to go for bust tomorrow and charge for Whitby, about 40 miles distant. I might even get the further twenty miles home with an early enough start and if the patch held.

I got 30 miles the next day, moving into the North Yorkshire Moors National Park, passing the hilltop Captain Cook Monument and iconic Roseberry Topping before two additional blowouts and continuous resultant punctures made further progress impossible past Kildale. Lesson learned: always have a spare tyre and tubes. I called in the cavalry 28 miles from home, and, rather embarrassingly, my dad came to pick me up. That embarrassment in itself, however, shows I have a long way to go with my ego management.

Aside from the tyre and inner situation, I discovered a number of other issues on this initial leg of my global tour.

1. I need spares for things that will break, specifically the trailer arm pivot pin, and also, intuitively, the rear wheel skewer which the trailer arms hook on to. It came with the trailer, and seemed outrageously flimsy. But as the trailer was cheap, around forty quid, I bought another one for spares, and also resolved to make additional skewers and pivot pins from galvanized or stainless steel threaded rod because it wouldn't cost much and could quite

possibly save my life. Parts of the trailer had already started to rust, too.

2. I needn't bring my large rucksack rather than the trailer bag, because I never used it, and it's lack of waterproofing was a liability, even with its rain cover. I resolved to buy a waterproof duffel bag instead, which would allow similar if not greater volume and far easier access to the contents.

3. Larger, waterproof panniers, because you can never have too much space to put stuff.

4. A bigger, better tent with roomier vestibules for gear and cooking.

5. A larger handlebar bag.

6. A better, more robust camera.

Everything else worked great.

An astrophysicist once told me (and I listened closely because she had magnificent breasts), if you hold aloft a grain of sand at arm's length and close one eye, the area of sky covered by that grain of sand contains two thousand galaxies, each one consisting of hundreds of billions of stars. Think about that for a second. *Thousands of trillions* of stars, one grain of sand, great tits. I've thought a lot about those boobs while I've stared at the night sky from my tent, far from light pollution, pondering the small and the vast, the round and the heavy.

When one considers we're no more than microbes on a dust mote, hurtling through space at a couple of million miles an hour, as part of one of *two hundred billion* star systems in our galaxy alone (or one hundred billion, or three hundred billion, depending on who you listen to. Let's just say 'lots'). Which in turn, is one of *hundreds of billions* of galaxies, you'll find we're so insignificant, so bacterial, dividing ourselves into cultural groups is so meaningless it's beyond puerile. Creating arbitrary differences in an attempt to establish a social hierarchy (because that's what it is, let's be honest) is possibly the dumbest, most self-aggrandizing thing we can do. Yet we do it.

Which of course means cultures are a load of bollocks. They really are. Our cultures are indulgent artifice. Peripheral scrollwork. Which means I respect individual cultural mores because I'm being polite, not because they deserve respect. Your culture is something *you* deem important, when it clearly, objectively, is not. I can appreciate beauty and artistry, of course: I'm not a barbarian, but I draw the line way before the genital mutilation of children, for example.

And the irony is here I am travelling the world with the intent of experiencing these various cultures. Why? The real answer is it's the only thing we *can* do as individuals to meagerly expand our microcosmic experience. It's the ultimate earthbound odyssey, but in the broad perspective it's titchy and means little more than nothing.

So why bother doing anything, if we're so insignificant? That's a very good question. I say because we're here. I didn't choose to be alive, but I'm here now, and I need to do *something*, to entertain myself if nothing else. May as well, right? If the mumbling kiddie-fiddlers who don't pay taxes are correct, and consciousness is immortal (which is highly unlikely), then we're off somewhere else once we shuffle off the material, so I fully intend to enjoy this bit while I can. I can't imagine a worse thing in the world than dying with regret, and that's where I was heading.

So call it a mid-life crisis, or a descent into abject irresponsibility, or my favourite: detaching myself from the real world. A close friend of mine asked me what I was running from: I don't think I'm running from anything, I think I'm running *towards* something.

What that thing is, however, remains to be seen.

Printed in Poland
by Amazon Fulfillment
Poland Sp. z o.o., Wrocław